AMERICAN POLITICAL, ECONOMIC, AND SECURITY ISSUES

AMERICAN SAMOA: FEDERAL LAW AND COURT ISSUES

American Political, Economic, and Security Issues

Additional books in this series can be found on Nova's website under the Series tab.

Additional E-books in this series can be found on Nova's website under the E-book tab.

Laws and Legislation

Additional books in this series can be found on Nova's website under the Series tab.

Additional E-books in this series can be found on Nova's website under the E-book tab.

AMERICAN POLITICAL, ECONOMIC, AND SECURITY ISSUES

AMERICAN SAMOA: FEDERAL LAW AND COURT ISSUES

LUCAS G. RAMOS
EDITOR

Nova Science Publishers, Inc.
New York

For permission to use material from this book please contact us:
Telephone 631-231-7269; Fax 631-231-8175
Web Site: http://www.novapublishers.com

LIBRARY OF CONGRESS CATALOGING-IN-PUBLICATION DATA

American samoa : federal law and court issues / editors, Lucas G. Ramos.
p. cm.
Includes index.
ISBN 978-1-61761-938-0 (hardcover)
1. Law--American Samoa. 2. Courts--American Samoa. 3. American Samoa--Politics and government. I. Ramos, Lucas G.
KVH6.3.A44 2010
349.961'3--dc22

2010037333

Published by Nova Science Publishers, Inc. † New York

CONTENTS

PREFACE

Because American Samoa does not have a federal court like the CNMI, Guam or USVI, matters of federal law arising in American Samoa have generally been adjudicated in U.S. district courts in Hawaii or the District of Columbia. Reasons offered for changing the existing system focus primarily on the difficulties of adjudicating matters of federal law arising in American Samoa, principally based on American Samoa's remote location, and the desire to provide American Samoans more direct access to justice. This book discusses the current system of adjudicating matters of federal law in American Samoa and how it compares to those in the Commonwealth of the Northern Mariana Islands (CNMI), Guam and the U.S. Virgin Islands (USVI), and the reasons for or against changing the current system with potential scenarios and issues associated with establishing a federal court there.

Chapter 1- American Samoa is the only populated U.S. insular area that does not have a federal court. Congress has granted the local High Court federal jurisdiction for certain federal matters, such as specific areas of maritime law. GAO was asked to conduct a study of American Samoa's system for addressing matters of federal law. Specifically, this report discusses: (1) the current system for adjudicating matters of federal law in American Samoa and how it compares to those in the Commonwealth of the Northern Mariana Islands (CNMI), Guam, and the U.S. Virgin Islands (USVI); (2) the reasons offered for or against changing the current system for adjudicating matters of federal law in American Samoa; (3) potential scenarios and issues associated with establishing a federal court in American Samoa or expanding the federal jurisdiction of the local court; and (4) the potential cost elements and funding sources associated with implementing those different scenarios. To conduct this work, the authors reviewed previous studies and testimonies, and collected information from and conducted interviews with federal government officials and American Samoa government officials.

Chapter 2 – These remarks were delievered as testimony. President Lolo M. Mogliga, before the House Subcommittee on Insular Affiars.

Chapter 3 – These remarks were delievered as testimony. Savali Talavou Ale, Speaker of the House of Representatives, before the United States House of Representative's Subcommittee on Insular Affairs.

Chapter 4 – This is a statement of Stephen Sander, Acting Director, Office of Insular Affairs, Department of the Interior, before the Subcommittee on Insular Affairs, House Committee on Natural Resources, regarding Federal Court Options for American Samoa.

In: American Samoa: Federal Law and Court… ISBN: 978-1-61761-938-0
Editor: Lucas G. Ramos

Chapter 1

American Samoa: Issues Associated with Potential Changes to the Current System for Adjudicating Matters of Federal Law

United States Government Accountability Office

Why GAO Did This Study

American Samoa is the only populated U.S. insular area that does not have a federal court. Congress has granted the local High Court federal jurisdiction for certain federal matters, such as specific areas of maritime law. GAO was asked to conduct a study of American Samoa's system for addressing matters of federal law. Specifically, this report discusses: (1) the current system for adjudicating matters of federal law in American Samoa and how it compares to those in the Commonwealth of the Northern Mariana Islands (CNMI), Guam, and the U.S. Virgin Islands (USVI); (2) the reasons offered for or against changing the current system for adjudicating matters of federal lawin American Samoa; (3) potential scenarios and issues associated with establishing a federal court in American Samoa or expanding the federal jurisdiction of the local court; and (4) the potential cost elements and funding sources associated with implementing those different scenarios. To conduct this work, we reviewed previous studies and testimonies, and collected information from and conducted interviews with federal government officials and American Samoa government officials.

What GAO Recommends

This report contains no recommendations, but is focused on providing decision makers with further details on various scenarios for potentially changing the current system of adjudicating matters of federal law in American Samoa.

What GAO Found

Because American Samoa does not have a federal court like the CNMI, Guam, or USVI, matters of federal law arising in American Samoa have generally been adjudicated in U.S. district courts in Hawaii or the District of Columbia.

Reasons offered for changing the existing system focus primarily on the difficulties of adjudicating matters of federal law arising in American Samoa, principally based on American Samoa's remote location, and the desire to provide American Samoans more direct access to justice. Reasons offered against any changes focus primarily on concerns about the effects of an increased federal presence on Samoan culture and traditions and concerns about juries' impartiality given close family ties. During the mid-1990s, several proposals were studied and many of the issues discussed then, such as the protection of local culture, were also raised during this study.

Based on previous studies and information gathered for this report, GAO identified three potential scenarios, if changes were to be made: (1) establish a federal court in American Samoa under Article IV of the U.S. Constitution, (2) establish a district court in American Samoa as a division of the District of Hawaii, or (3) expand the federal jurisdiction of the High Court of American Samoa. Each scenario would present unique issues to be addressed, such as what jurisdiction to grant the court.

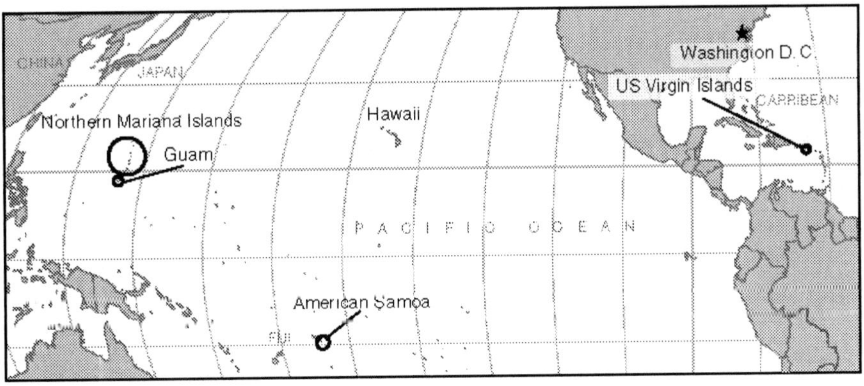

Source: GAO, Map Resources (map art).

Map Showing Location of American Samoa, CNMI, Guam, and USVI

The potential cost elements for establishing a federal court in American Samoa include agency rental costs, personnel costs, and operational costs, most of which would be funded by congressional appropriations. Exact details of the costs to be incurred would have to be determined when, and if, any of the scenarios were adopted. The controversy surrounding whether and how to create a venue for adjudicating matters of federal law in American Samoa is not principally focused on an analysis of cost effectiveness, but other policy considerations, such as equity, justice, and cultural preservation.

ABBREVIATIONS

AOUSC	Administrative Office of the U.S. Courts
CJA	Criminal Justice Act
CNMI	Commonwealth of the Northern Mariana Islands
DOI	Department of the Interior
DOJ	Department of Justice
EOUSA	Executive Office for U.S. Attorneys
FBI	Federal Bureau of Investigation
GSA	General Services Administration
USMS	U.S. Marshals Service
USVI	U.S. Virgin Islands

June 27, 2008

The Honorable Nick J. Rahall II
Chairman
The Honorable Don Young
Ranking Republican Member
Committee on Natural Resources
House of Representatives

The Honorable Eni F.H. Faleomavaega
House of Representatives

American Samoa is unique among U.S. insular areas in that it does not have a federal court.[1] A U.S. territory since the early 1900s, American Samoa has internal self-government under a locally adopted Constitution, and the High Court of American Samoa is not part of the U.S. federal judicial structure. American Samoa's local judiciary was initially created and administered by the U.S. Navy, but since 1951 has operated under the authority of the Secretary of the Interior, who appoints the High Court Chief Justice and Associate Justice.

The issue of establishing a federal court in American Samoa is not new. In the mid-1990s, legislative proposals were developed that would have included the establishment of a federal court in American Samoa. However, these initiatives were not enacted by Congress and were controversial among American Samoans. Then, again, in February 2006, the Delegate from American Samoa introduced legislation in the U.S. Congress to establish a federal court in American Samoa[2] and later that month, the American Samoa legislature held a public hearing to solicit public comments.[3] No congressional actions were taken on the bill and the Delegate from American Samoa withdrew the legislation after he and others requested this report.

In particular, you requested that we examine the unique judicial structure of American Samoa and identify the issues associated with establishing a federal court in American Samoa. This report discusses:

(1) the current system and structure for adjudicating matters of federal law arising in American Samoa and how it compares to those in the Commonwealth of the Northern Mariana Islands (CNMI), Guam, and the U.S. Virgin Islands (USVI);

(2) the reasons that have been offered for or against changing the current system and structure for adjudicating matters of federal law in American Samoa;
(3) the description of different scenarios for establishing a federal court in American Samoa or expanding the federal jurisdiction of the High Court of American Samoa if a change to the current system were made, and the identification of issues associated with each scenario; and,
(4) the potential cost elements and funding sources associated with implementing the different scenarios for establishing a federal court in American Samoa.

We are not making recommendations regarding whether the current system and structure for adjudicating matters of federal law in American Samoa should be changed. Also, we will not be making any determinations as to whether the current system is more or less costly than the different scenarios presented in this report. Rather, our purpose is to provide decision makers with information regarding the issues associated with potential scenarios for change.

To meet our objectives, we reviewed historical documents, congressional testimonies, law review articles, and previous studies, and conducted interviews with federal government officials, to include: the Administrative Office of the U.S. Courts (AOUSC); the Department of the Interior (DOI); the Department of Justice (DOJ); the General Services Administration (GSA); the U.S. Attorneys offices serving federal courts located in CNMI and Guam, Hawaii, and USVI; the Inspector General offices of the Departments of Education, Homeland Security, Transportation, and Health and Human Services; the U.S. Court of Appeals for the Ninth Circuit; the U.S. District Court of Hawaii; the District Court for the Northern Mariana Islands; the District Court of Guam; and the District Court of the Virgin Islands. We also reviewed historical documents and court statistical data from and conducted interviews with American Samoa government officials in the legislative, judicial, and executive branches of government. In addition, to address the first three objectives, we held group discussions with members of the local bar association and the local chamber of commerce, and conducted a public forum with college students and members of the general public during our visit to American Samoa in October 2007. Further, we established an e-mail account and received comments from the general public regarding their views on possible scenarios for establishing a federal court in American Samoa or expanding the federal jurisdiction of the High Court of American Samoa. Although these views cannot be generalized to the population of American Samoa as a whole, they provided us with a better understanding of the range of issues that were important to members of the local community. To address the first three objectives, we also interviewed recognized legal experts on territorial governance issues. These experts were not intended to be representative of all expert opinions on American Samoa judicial issues, but were contacted because they could provide insights on territorial governance issues in general. For the fourth objective, we collected available data regarding the potential cost elements and funding sources related to establishing a federal court in American Samoa from AOUSC, GSA, and DOJ's Executive Office for United States Attorneys (EOUSA) and U.S. Marshals Service (USMS). Since these agencies could only provide rough estimates of potential costs, and because of the numerous caveats associated with the various costs elements, the data cannot be used for budget purposes or to measure the true costs regarding the establishment of a federal court in American Samoa. Further, since the court scenarios were hypothetical and the exact details of the jurisdiction, staffing, and physical facilities are not known, the estimated costs cannot be aggregated to obtain a precise estimate of the total costs for the scenarios. We did not collect any cost data related to expanding the federal jurisdiction of the High Court of American Samoa, since this would be a unique judicial structure and there is no comparable existing federal court structure upon which to estimate costs. We found the cost data provided to be sufficiently reliable to provide rough estimates of potential future costs for establishing a federal court in American Samoa, with limitations as noted. Appendix I contains a more detailed description of the scope and methodology.

We conducted this performance audit from April 2007 to June 2008 in accordance with generally accepted government auditing standards. Those standards require that we plan and perform the audit to obtain sufficient, appropriate evidence to provide a reasonable basis for our findings and conclusions based on our audit objectives. We believe that the evidence obtained provides a reasonable basis for our findings and conclusions based on our audit objectives.

RESULTS IN BRIEF

In contrast to other insular areas of the United States, such as CNMI, Guam, and USVI, which have their own federal courts, American Samoa does not have a federal court; rather, the High Court of American Samoa has been granted limited federal jurisdiction for certain issues, such as food safety, protection of animals, conservation, and shipping issues. Because of the limits to the High Court's federal jurisdiction, other matters of federal law arising in American Samoa have been adjudicated in U.S. district courts, mainly in Hawaii or the District of Columbia. Since a 2001 precedent-setting case involving human trafficking, federal prosecutors have initiated criminal proceedings in the U.S. District Court of Hawaii, in addition to past practices of handling matters only in the U.S. District Court for the District of Columbia. With regard to federal civil cases, in certain circumstances, such as when both the plaintiff and the defendant reside in American Samoa and the events giving rise to the civil action occurred in American Samoa, there is no federal court with jurisdiction to handle such matters.

Reasons offered for changing the existing system focus primarily on the difficulties of adjudicating matters of federal law arising in American Samoa, such as logistical challenges related to American Samoa's remote location, along with the goal of providing residents with more direct access to justice in their place of residence, while reasons offered against changing the current system of adjudicating matters of federal law focus largely on concerns about the impact of an increased federal presence on Samoan culture and traditions, as well as concerns regarding the impartiality of local juries given close family ties. During the mid-1990s, several proposals for changing the current system for adjudicating matters of federal law were studied and many of the issues discussed at that time, such as protecting local culture and traditions, were also raised during our study.

Based on these studies and information gathered for this chapter, we identified three principal scenarios for change, if a change to the current system were made:(1) establishing a district court in American Samoa pursuant to Article IV of the U.S. Constitution,[4] (2) establishing a district court in American Samoa that would be a division of the District of Hawaii, or (3) expanding the federal jurisdiction of the High Court of American Samoa. Key issues associated with implementing any of these scenarios include the need for enacting a statutory change and overcoming operational challenges, such as what jurisdiction to grant the court and what type of courthouse and detention facility would need to be built under each scenario.

The potential cost elements for establishing a federal court in American Samoa under the first two scenarios include court construction and agency rental costs, as well as personnel and operational costs for judicial and executive branch staff, most of which would be funded by direct appropriations to each federal agency. However, the estimated cost elements for these two scenarios are based on assumptions that could change in actual implementation and the exact details of the jurisdiction, staffing, and physical facilities would have to be determined if, and when, any of the scenarios were adopted. Therefore, the cost elements presented cannot be used for budget purposes and an analysis of cost effectiveness for individual scenarios would be of limited value given the data limitations. Regarding the third scenario, we did not collect cost data because the granting of federal criminal jurisdiction and expanded federal civil jurisdiction to the local High Court would be a unique judicial arrangement, and there is no existing federal structure upon which federal agencies could base cost estimates. However, the controversy surrounding whether and how to create a venue for adjudicating matters of federal law in American Samoa is not principally focused on costs, but on other factors, such as equity, justice, and cultural preservation. Thus policy considerations, other than an analysis of cost effectiveness, are more likely to be the basis for deciding whether and how to establish a court with federal jurisdiction in American Samoa.

In May 2008, we requested comments on a draft of this report from the Administrative Office of the U.S. Courts; the Department of the Interior; the Department of Justice; the General Services Administration; and officials representing the executive, legislative, and judicial branches of the government of American Samoa. The Administrative Office of the U.S. Courts and the Department of Justice provided technical comments which we have incorporated into this chapter as appropriate. In addition to the technical comments received, the Administrative Office of the U.S. Courts, the Department of the Interior, and the Office of the Governor of American Samoa provided official letters for inclusion in this chapter. These letters can be seen in appendixes II, III, and IV, respectively.

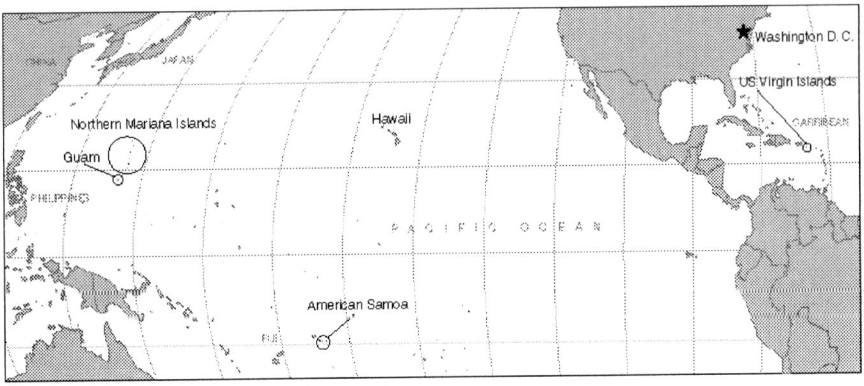

Source: GAO, Map Resources (map art).

Figure 1. Map Showing the Location of American Samoa, CNMI, Guam, and USVI

BACKGROUND

As shown in figure 1, of the four insular areas addressed in this chapter, three are located in the Pacific—American Samoa, CNMI, and Guam—and one is located in the Caribbean—the USVI. Each of these insular areas has its own unique culture and historical relationship with the United States. See appendices V, VI, VII, and VIII for detailed descriptions of the history and development of the judicial systems of American Samoa, CNMI, Guam, and USVI, respectively.

American Samoa, the only U.S. insular area in the southern hemisphere, is located about 2,600 miles southwest of Hawaii. American Samoa consists of five volcanic islands and two coral atolls, covering a land area of 76 square miles, slightly larger than Washington, D.C. The capital of American Samoa, Pago Pago, is located on the main island of Tutuila, which is mostly rugged terrain with relatively little level land. Agricultural production is limited by the scarcity of arable land, and tourism is impaired by the island's remote location and lack of tourist-rated facilities. Two tuna canneries constitute the main sources of private sector employment. Most of the economic activity and government operations on Tutuila take place in the Pago Pago Bay area.

According to the American Samoa Department of Commerce data, in 2005 the population of American Samoa was about 65,500.[5] Unlike residents born in CNMI, Guam, and USVI, residents born in American Samoa are nationals of the United States, but may become naturalized U.S. citizens.[6]Like residents of the other insular areas, residents of American Samoa have many of the rights of citizens of the 50 states, but cannot vote in U.S. national elections and do not have voting representation in the final approval of legislation by the full Congress. The Delegate from American Samoa has all congressional privileges, including a vote in committee, except a vote in Congress as a whole. Further, according to Census Bureau data for 2000, the median household income in American Samoa was $18,200, less than half of the U.S. median household income of almost $41,000.

American Samoa does not have an organic act that formally establishes the relationship between American Samoa and the United States. Two deeds of cession were initially completed between Samoan chiefs, or *matai*, and the United States in 1900 and 1904[7] and ratified by the federal government in 1929.[8] In these deeds, the United States pledged to promote peace and welfare, to establish a good and sound government, and to preserve the rights and property of the people. The U.S. Navy was initially responsible for federal governance of the territory. Then, in 1951, federal governance was transferred to the Secretary of the Interior, which continues today. The Secretary exercises broad powers with regard to American Samoa, including "all civil, judicial, and military powers" of government in American Samoa.[9] American Samoa has had its own constitution since 1960, and since 1983, the local American Samoa constitution may only be amended by an act of Congress.[10]

The American Samoa Constitution provides for three separate branches of government—the executive, the legislative, and the judicial. Since 1977, a popularly elected Governor heads the American Samoa executive branch for 4-year terms.[11] Nearly 40 American Samoa departments, offices, and other entities within the executive branch of the American Samoa government provide public safety, public works, education, health, commerce, and other services. The Governor has responsibility for appointing the Attorney General, Director of Public Safety, and other executive branch agency leaders. The legislature, or *Fono*, is comprised of 18 senators and 20 representatives. Each of the senators is elected in accordance with Samoan custom by the city councils of the counties that the senator represents. Each of the representatives is popularly elected from the representative districts. American Samoa exercises authority over its immigration system through its own locally adopted laws. In fiscal year 2007, a total of almost $105 million in federal funds were provided from a variety of federal agencies, including the Departments of the Interior, Education, Agriculture, Transportation, and Health and Human Services. Specifically, DOI provided funds that same year in the amount of $22.9 million for American Samoa government operations, including the High Court of American Samoa. In addition to these federal funds, a portion of the funding for American Samoa government operations comes from local revenues.

American Samoa Judiciary

The American Samoa judiciary, as provided in the American Samoa Constitution and Samoan Code, consists of a High Court and a local district court under the administration and supervision of the Chief Justice.[12] The High Court consists of four divisions—the trial division; the family, drug, and alcohol division; the land and titles division; and the appellate division.[13] The trial division, which consists of the Chief Justice, the Associate Justice, and associate judges, is a court of general jurisdiction, empowered to hear, among other things, felony cases and civil cases in which the amount in controversy exceeds $5,000. The Chief Justice and the Associate Justice are appointed by the U.S. Secretary of the Interior and are required to be trained in the law. There are six associate judges, who are appointed by the Governor and are not required to have legal training. The associate judges are *matai*, or chiefs, and they preside over cases in the High Court, playing a more significant role in deciding issues of *matai* titles and land. There is one local district court judge, who is appointed by the Governor and must also have legal training, who hears matters such as misdemeanor criminal offenses and civil cases in which the matter in controversy does not exceed $5,000.[14] The Chief and Associate Justices, and the local district and associate judges hold office for life with good behavior.[15] The American Samoa judiciary has a public defender, probation officers, translators, and marshals. Since the 1970s the Secretary of the Interior has appointed federal judges, usually from the Ninth Circuit, to serve temporarily as Acting Associate Justices in the appellate division of the High Court of American Samoa.[16]

American Samoan Customs and Traditions

American Samoan customs and traditions have an influence over the local legal system. The distinctive Samoan way of life, or *fa'a Samoa,* is deeply imbedded in traditional American Samoa history and culture. *Fa'a Samoa* is organized around the concept of extended family groups—people related by blood, marriage, or adoption—or *aiga.* Family members acknowledge allegiance to the island leader hierarchy comprised of family leaders, or *matai* (chiefs). *Matai* are responsible for the welfare of their respective *aiga* and play a central role in protecting and allocating family lands. About 90 percent of land in American Samoa is communally owned and controlled by *matai*, and there are limits in American Samoa law regarding the transfer of property.[17] The concept of *fa'a Samoa* extends to the governance structures in American Samoa and, thus, most high-ranking government officials, including judges, are *matai.* Further, Samoan law allows for a custom of *ifoga*, or ceremonial apology, whereby if a member of one family commits an offense against a member of another family, the family of the offender proceeds to the headquarters of the family of the offended person and asks for forgiveness. After appropriate confession of guilt and ceremonial contrition by the offending family, the family offended against can forgive the offense. If the offender is convicted in court, the court may reduce the sentence of the offender if it finds that an *ifoga* was performed.

Past Proposals to Establish a Federal Court in American Samoa

The issue of establishing a federal court in American Samoa is not new. This issue has arisen within the larger question of defining the political status of American Samoa and its relationship with the United States. For example, in the 1930s, Congress considered legislation that would provide an avenue of appeal from the High Court of American Samoa to the U.S. District Court of Hawaii, during its deliberation of an organic act for American Samoa. However, this initiative was not enacted by Congress. Further, since 1969, there have been three American Samoa commissions convened to study the future political status of American Samoa. These commissions have studied, among other things, the necessity of an organic act.[18] The most recent commission's report, published in January 2007, did not recommend any changes in American Samoa's political status as an unorganized and unincorporated territory of the United States, with the intent that American Samoa could continue to be a part of the United States and also have the freedom to preserve Samoan culture.[19] In addition, in the mid-1990s DOJ proposed legislative options for changing the judicial structure of American Samoa, including establishing a federal court within the territory. These proposals were developed in response to growing concerns involving white-collar crime in American Samoa, which were detailed in a December 1994

DOJ crime assessment report.[20] However, while the House Committee on Resources held hearings on the 1994 DOJ report in August 1995, and judicial committees studied various legislative options, the Congress did not take any actions on the proposals. Then, in February 2006, the Delegate from American Samoa introduced legislation in the U.S. Congress to establish a federal court in American Samoa and later that month, the American Samoa *Fono* held a joint legislative public hearing to solicit public comments on the bill.[21]No congressional actions were taken on the bill and the Delegate from American Samoa withdrew the legislation after he and others requested this report.

Table 1. Comparison between Article IV and Article III Courts

	Article IV courts in CNMI, Guam, and USVI	Article III courts
Jurisdiction	Federal and bankruptcy combined	Federal and bankruptcy separate
Judges' terms	10-year term, President may remove for cause	Life, for good behavior
Judges' salaries	Set by statute	Constitutionally protected
Judges' responsibilities	Cannot sit on U.S. Court of Appeals panel	May sit on U.S. Court of Appeals panel.
Judges' benefits	If the judge retires after meeting certain age and service requirements, the judge receives an annuity equal to the salary at the time of retirement with limited cost-of-living increases. The judgemay also take senior status[a]after meeting the age andservice requirements and ifrecalled by the chief judge of the circuit to perform judicial duties, in which case the judge would receive the salary of an active judge. An annuity may be available to those judges who left office prior to retirement. Federal life insurance benefits are not offered.	If the judge retires after meeting certain age and service requirements, the judge receives an annuity equal to the judge's salary at the time of retirement. The judge may also take senior status after meeting the age and service requirements and receive the salary of an active district judge, provided that certain workload requirements are met. Federal life insurance benefits are offered throughout a judge's tenure.

Table 1. (Continued)

	Article IV courts in CNMI, Guam, and USVI	Article III courts
Judges' appointment	President with advice and consent of the Senate.	President with advice and consent of the Senate.
Designation of others in judges' absence	The chief judge from the respective circuit or the Chief Justice of the United States can temporarily designate others to handle court matters, including other Article IV judges, Article III judges, or judges from the local superior or local supreme court.	The chief judge from the circuit court can temporarily designate only other Article III judges from within the circuit to handle court matters; the Chief Justice of the United States can assign Article III judges from outside the circuit to handle court matters.

Source: GAO analysis of relevant federal laws.

[a]Senior status is a form of semiretirement for federal judges in which, after meeting certain age and service requirements, a judge may work part-time and receive the salary of an active judge.

Differences between Article IV Courts in Insular Areas and Article III Courts

The federal courts in the insular areas of CNMI, Guam, and USVI were established under Article IV of the Constitution, whereas U.S. district courts elsewhere in the United States were established under Article III of the Constitution.[22] Article IV courts are similar to Article III courts, but differ in terms of specific jurisdiction and tenure of the judges. As shown in table 1, Article IV courts generally exercise the same jurisdiction as Article III courts and may also exercise jurisdiction over local matters. Article IV judges are appointed by the President, with the advice and consent of the Senate, serve terms of 10 years, and can be removed by the President for cause. Article III judges are appointed by the President, with the advice and consent of the Senate, and serve with Article III protections of life tenure for good behavior and immunity from reductions in salary. Article IV judges hear both federal and bankruptcy cases, whereas Article III courts generally have a separate unit to hear bankruptcy cases. An Article III judge can be designated by the Chief Judge of the Circuit Court of Appeals or the Chief Justice of the United States to sit on an Article IV court. However, an Article IV judge can be designated to sit only as a magistrate judge on an Article III court.[23]

The Federal Courts in CNMI, Guam, and USVI

The federal courts in CNMI, Guam, and USVI were established at different times, but developed in similar ways. The District Court for the Northern Mariana Islands was established in 1977 as specified in the 1975 agreement, or covenant, between the Northern Mariana Islands and the United States.[24] The District Court of Guam was established when the federal government passed an Organic Act for Guam in 1950.[25] The District Court of the Virgin Islands, as it currently exists, was established by an Organic Act in 1936.[26]Each of these federal courts initially had jurisdiction over federal, as well as local, issues. Over time, however, the federal courts were divested of jurisdiction over local issues, with the exception of the District Court of the Virgin Islands, which maintains jurisdiction over cases involving local offenses that have the same underlying facts as federal offenses.[27]Similarly, each of the federal courts had appellate jurisdiction over the local trial courts until the local government established a local appellate court. CNMI, Guam, and USVI have all established local Supreme Courts, so that the federal courts no longer have appellate jurisdiction over local cases. As such, the jurisdiction of each of the three federal courts currently resembles that of district courts of the United States, which include federal question jurisdiction, diversity jurisdiction, and the jurisdiction of a bankruptcy court.[28]Decisions of the District Court for the Northern Mariana Islands and the District Court of Guam may be appealed to the U.S. Court of Appeals for the Ninth Circuit, and decisions of the District Court of the Virgin Islands may be appealed to the U.S. Court of Appeals for the Third Circuit. An Article IV judge—two Article IV judges in the case of the Virgin Islands—sits on each of the federal courts and is appointed by the President with the advice and consent of the Senate, for a term of 10 years, but may be removed by the President for cause. For the history and development of courts in the CNMI, Guam, and USVI, see appendixes VI, VII, and VIII, respectively.

Unlike Other Insular Areas, Matters of Federal Law in American Samoa Are Adjudicated in U.S. District Courts in Hawaii or the District of Columbia

Unlike other insular areas, such as CNMI, Guam, and USVI, American Samoa does not have a federal court. As a result, federal law enforcement officials have pursued violations of federal criminal law arising in American Samoa in the U.S. district courts in Hawaii or the District of Columbia. In the absence of a federal court in American Samoa, federal law has provided federal jurisdiction to the High Court of American Samoa in areas such as food safety and shipping issues, which is quite narrow compared to the comprehensive federal jurisdiction granted to federal courts in other insular areas.

American Samoa's Local Judicial Structure Differs from Local Judicial Structures in CNMI, Guam, and USVI

With regard to its local judicial structure, American Samoa is different from other U.S. insular areas. The judicial system in American Samoa consists only of local courts that handle limited federal matters, whereas the judicial system in CNMI, Guam, and USVI are composed of local courts and federal courts that operate independently from each other. Also, whereas the justices of the High Court in American Samoa are appointed by the Secretary of the Interior, the judges of the local courts in CNMI, Guam, and USVI are appointed by the Governors of each insular area. Further, although decisions of the appellate division of the High Court of American Samoa have been appealed to the Secretary of the Interior, federal law provides that, 15 years after the establishment of a local appellate court, decisions of the local appellate courts in CNMI, Guam, and USVI may be appealed to the U.S. Supreme Court.[29]

Because there is no federal court in American Samoa, matters of federal law arising in American Samoa have generally been adjudicated in either the District of Hawaii (Honolulu, Hawaii) or the District of Columbia (Washington, D.C.), as stated earlier.

Table 2. Comparison of Local (Nonfederal) Courts in American Samoa, CNMI, Guam, and USVI

	American Samoa				
		High Court			
	Local District Court	**Trial Division**	**Land and Titles Division**	**Family, Drug, andAlcohol Division**	**Appellate Division**
Jurisdiction	Minor criminal andcivil cases[a]	Major criminal and civil cases[b]	Land and titles cases	Juvenile, cert-aindomestic relations,dom-estic violence, and certain substance and alcohol abuse cases	Appellate jurisdiction over district court,and trial, land andtitles, and family, drug, and alcohol divisions
Rights of appeal	High Court Trial orAppellate Division	High Court Appellate Division	High Court Appellate Division	High Court Appellate Division	Secretary of theInterior
Judges' appoint-ment	Governor, uponrecommendati on ofChief Justice andconfirmation by localSenate	Justices: Secretaryof the Interior;Associate judges: Governor, uponrecommendatio n of Chief Justice and confirmation by local Senate	Justices: Secretary of the Interior;Associate judges:Governor, upon recommendation of Chief Justice and confirmation by local Senate	Justices: Secre-taryof the Interior;Associate judges:Governor, uponrecommendatio n ofChief Justice andconfirmation by local Senate	Justices: Secretaryof the Interior; Associate judges:Governor, upon recommendation ofChief Justice and confirmation by local Senate[g]

Table 2. (Continued)

	American Samoa				
	Local District Court	High Court			
		Trial Division	Land and Titles Division	Family, Drug, and Alcohol Division	Appellate Division
Judges' term	Life, but may be removed by Chief Justice for cause	Justices: Life, but may be removed bySecretary of the Interior for cause; Associate judges: Life, but may be removed by Chief Justice for cause	Justices: Life, but may be removed by Secretary of theInterior for cause; Associate judges:Life, but may beremoved by ChiefJustice for cause	Justices: Life, but may be removed by Secretary of the Interior for cau-se; Associate judges: Life, but may be removed by Chief Justice for cause	Justices: Life, but may be removed by Secretary of the Interior for cause; Associate judges: Life, but may be removed by Chief Justice for cause
CNMI		**Guam**		**USVI**	
Superior Court[c]	**Supreme Court**	**Superior Court[d]**	**Supreme Court**	**Superior Court[e]**	**Supreme Court**
Original jurisdiction overcriminal and civilcases	Appellate jurisdiction over Superior Court decisions	Original juris-diction over criminal and civil cases	Appellate jurisdiction over Superior Court decisions	Original jurisdi-ction over criminal and civil cases	Appellate jurisdiction over Superior Court decisions
Supreme Court of CNMI	U.S. Supreme Court	Supreme Court of Guam	U.S. Supreme Court	Supreme Court of USVI	U.S. Court of Ap-peals for the Third Circuitf
Governor, with the advice and consent of the local Senate	Governor, with the advice and consent of the local Senate	Governor, with the advice and consent of the local legislature	Governor, with the advice and consent of the local legislature	Governor, with the advice and consent of the local legislature	Governor, with the advice and consent of the local legislature

Table 2. (Continued)

CNMI		Guam		USVI	
Superior Court[c]	Supreme Court	Superior Court[d]	Supreme Court	Superior Court[e]	Supreme Court
6 years, and may be reapoin-ted for 12-year terms	6 years, and may be reappointed for 12-year terms	7 years, and may be elected to subsequent terms, but may be removed for cause	10 years, and may be elected to subsequent terms, but may be removed for cause	6 years, unless sooner retired or removed for cause	10 years, and may be reapointed for life term, but may be retired or removed for cause

Source: GAO analysis of relevant federal, American Samoa, CNMI, Guam, and USVI laws.

[a]Minor criminal and civil cases include cases such as misdemeanor criminal cases and civil cases in which the amount in controversy does not exceed $5,000.

[b]Major criminal and civil cases include cases such as felony criminal cases and civil cases in which the amount in controversy exceeds $5,000.

[c]The Superior Court of CNMI has a family court division.

[d]The Superior Court of Guam has traffic, small claims, family, and drug court divisions.

[e]The Superior Court of USVI consists of criminal, civil, traffic, family, conciliation, and small claims divisions.

[f]The U.S. Court of Appeals for the Third Circuit has appellate jurisdiction over decisions of the Supreme Court of the Virgin Islands for the first 15 years after its establishment. After the first 15 years, in 2022, the U.S. Supreme Court will have appellate jurisdiction over decisions of the Supreme Court of the Virgin Islands.

[g]The quorum for the appellate division is two High Court justices and one associate judge. Since there are only two High Court justices and one of those justices has usually been involved in the matter in the lower courts, the Secretary of the Interior has used the practice of appointing active or senior federal district judges, usually from the Ninth Circuit, as acting associate justices of the High Court, who travel to American Samoa to hear matters before the High Court Appellate Division as needed.

Federal Criminal Cases Arising in American Samoa Are Generally Heard in Hawaii and the District of Columbia

With regard to criminal matters, although federal criminal law extends to American Samoa, questions surrounding the proper jurisdiction and venue of cases have posed complex legal issues when violations of federal law occurred solely in American Samoa.[30] However, since a 2001 precedent-setting case involving human trafficking,[31] DOJ prosecutors told us that some of the legal issues regarding jurisdiction and venue that had been unsettled in the past have been resolved. For example, federal law provides that the proper venue for a criminal case involving a federal crime committed outside of a judicial district is: (1) the district in which the defendant is arrested or first brought; or (2) if the defendant is not yet arrested or first brought to a district, in the judicial district of the defendant's last known residence; or (3) if no such residence is known, in the U.S. District Court for the District of Columbia.[32]

Prior to this 2001 case, most cases arising in American Samoa were brought in the U.S. District Court for the District of Columbia. In this 2001 case, prosecutors used the "first brought" statute to establish venue in the District of Hawaii, since the defendant was arrested and "first brought" to Hawaii and then indicted in the District of Hawaii. Based on the facts and arguments presented, the Ninth Circuit upheld this application of the "first brought" statute.[33] Following this case, most defendants who have been charged with committing federal offenses in American Samoa have been charged in one of two venues—the U.S. district courts in Hawaii or the District of Columbia, because there is no federal court in American Samoa.[34] In 2006 and 2007, DOJ attorneys prosecuted defendants in the U.S. district courts in both Hawaii and the District of Columbia for civil rights violations and public corruption cases arising in American Samoa.[35] DOJ prosecutors told us that their approach is adjusted depending on the facts of each case, legal challenges presented, and prosecutorial resources available.

Proper Federal Venue May Not Exist for the Adjudication of Certain Federal Civil and Bankruptcy Matters

With regard to certain federal civil matters, when both the plaintiff and the defendant reside in American Samoa, and the events giving rise to the civil action occurred in American Samoa, there may be no proper federal venue, meaning there may be no federal court that may hear the case.[36] However, some civil cases have been brought against the Secretary of the Department of the Interior alleging that the Secretary's administration of the government of American Samoa violated the U.S. Constitution.[37] In such cases, the U.S. District Court for the District of Columbia has been the appropriate forum, given that DOI is headquartered in Washington, D.C.

Table 3. Federal Statutes Conferring Jurisdiction on the High Court of American Samoa

U.S. Code and Title	Description
Title 7, Agriculture Chapter 3	Jurisdiction over cases arising under the U.S. Grain Standards Act.
Title 7, Agriculture Chapter 6	To enforce, prevent, and restrain violations of certain provisions related to insecticides and environmental pesticide control.
Title 7, Agriculture Chapter 54	To enforce, prevent, and restrain violations of certain provisions regarding the transportation, sale, and handling of certain animals.
Title 7, Agriculture Chapter 104	Jurisdiction over all cases arising under the Plant Protection Act regarding plant health.
Title 7, Agriculture Chapter 109	Jurisdiction over all cases arising under certain provisions regarding the protection of animal health.
Title 15, Commerce and Trade Chapter 44	To enforce, prevent, and restrain violations of certain provisions related to the protection of horses.
Title 16, Conservation Chapter 1	Exclusive jurisdiction to determine the payments that should be disbursed to villages and families located within the boundaries of the National Park ofAmerican Samoa for the lease of their land by the United States.
Title 21, Food and Drugs Chapter 10 and 12	To enforce, prevent, and restrain violations of certain provisions related to poultry and meat inspection.
Title 46, Shipping	To enforce provisions related to maritime preferred mortgages and liens.[a]

Source: GAO analysis of relevant federal laws.

[a] Maritime preferred mortgages are vessel mortgages that meet certain filing requirements, and maritime liens are claims against vessels for nonpayment for goods and services provided to the vessel.

Table 4. Comparison of Federal Jurisdiction of the High Court of American Samoa with Federal Courts in CNMI, Guam, and USVI

	High Court of American Samoa	Federal courts		
		District Court for CNMI	District Court of Guam	District Court of USVI
Federal jurisdiction	Limited to some conservation, agriculture, food safety, and shipping issues.	Jurisdiction of a district court of the United States and a bankruptcy court.[a]	Jurisdiction of a district court of the United States and a bankruptcy court.	Jurisdiction of a district court of the United States and a bankruptcy court; jurisdiction over all matters relat-ing to income tax laws applicable to the Virgin Islands; jurisdictionover local offenses with the same underlying facts as federaloffenses.
Rights of appeal	(1) Appellate Division of High Court, (2) Secretaryof the Interior, (3) U.S. Dist-rict Court for the District of Columbia, (4)U.S. Court of the District of Columbia Circuit, and (5) U.S. Supreme Court.	(1) U.S. Court of Appealsfor the Ninth Circuit, (2)U.S. Supreme Court.	(1) U.S. Court of Appeals for the Ninth Circuit, (2)U.S. Supreme Court.	(1) U.S. Court of Appealsfor the Third Circuit, (2)U.S. Supreme Court.
Judge appointment	Secretary of the Interior	President, with the advice and consent of the Senate	President, with the advice and consent of the Senate	President, with the advice and consent of the Senate

Table 4. (Continued)

	High Court of American Samoa	Federal courts		
		District Court for CNMI	District Court of Guam	District Court of USVI
Judge term	Life, but the Secretary of the Interior may remove for cause	10 years, but the President may remove for cause	10 years, but the President may remove for cause	10 years, but the President may remove for cause
Designation of others in judges' absence	The Secretary of the Interior can appoint Acting Associate Justices to sit on cases in the appellate division.	The chief judge of the Ninth Circuit can appoint a senior or active federal judge or judge from the local superior or supreme court, and the Chief Justice of the U.S. can appoint any district or circuit judge with consent.	The chief judge of the Ninth Circuit can appoint a senior or active federal judge or judge from the local superior or supreme court, and the Chief Justice of the United States can appoint any district or circuit judge with consent.	The chief judge of the Third Circuit can ap-point a senior or active federal judge or judge from the local superior or supreme court, and the Chief Justice of the United States can app-oint any district or circuit judge with consent.

Source: GAO analysis of relevant federal and American Samoa laws.

[a]The jurisdiction of U.S. district courts is prescribed in federal law and includes federal question jurisdiction, which is jurisdiction over civil cases arising under the U.S. Constitution, an act of Congress, or a treaty, and diversity jurisdiction, which is jurisdiction over civil cased filed based on the "diversity of citizenship" of the litigants, such as between citizens of different states or between U.S. citizens and those of another country, in which the matter in controversy has a sum or value that exceeds $75,000.

Bankruptcy relief is not available in American Samoa since federal law has not explicitly extended the U.S. Bankruptcy Code to American Samoa, and there is not a federal court in American Samoa in which bankruptcy claims may be adjudicated.[38] However, U.S. bankruptcy courts may exercise jurisdiction over petitions for relief filed by American Samoan entities under certain circumstances, such as if the entities reside or do business in a judicial district of the United States and the court finds that exercising jurisdiction would be in the best interest of the creditors and the debtors.

The Federal Jurisdiction of American Samoa's High Court is Very Limited Compared to Federal Courts in Other Insular Areas

As discussed above, because American Samoa does not have a federal court, federal officials have had to seek U.S. district courts to adjudicate matters of federal law arising in American Samoa. Despite the absence of a federal court in American Samoa, federal law provides that the local court—the High Court of American Samoa—has limited federal civil jurisdiction. In particular, federal law has explicitly granted the High Court of American Samoa federal jurisdiction for certain issues, such as food safety, protection of animals, conservation, and shipping issues, as shown in table 3. Although the High Court does not keep data on the number of federal cases it handles, the Chief Justice of the High Court official told us that, on occasion, these federal matters, particularly maritime cases,[39] have taken a significant amount of the court's time. The Chief Justice noted that the piecemeal nature of the High Court's federal jurisdiction sometimes creates challenges. For example, although the High Court has jurisdiction to hear certain maritime cases, the High Court does not have the authority under certain federal statutes to enjoin federal court proceedings or to transfer a case to a federal court. Such a situation may lead to parallel litigation in the High Court and a federal court.[40]

As shown in table 4, the federal jurisdiction of the High Court of American Samoa is very limited as compared to comprehensive federal jurisdiction in federal courts located in CNMI, Guam, and USVI. In addition to the limits of federal jurisdiction, there are differences in the way federal matters are heard in the High Court from the federal courts in other insular areas. For example, whereas the Secretary of the Interior asserts authority to review High Court decisions under federal law, the U.S. Courts of Appeals have appellate review of decisions of the federal courts in CNMI, Guam, and

USVI. Also, as stated earlier, whereas the Justices of the High Court are appointed by the Secretary of the Interior, the judges of the federal courts in CNMI, Guam, and USVI are appointed by the President, with the advice and consent of the U.S. Senate.

Proposals for Changing the Current System of Adjudicating Matters of Federal Law in American Samoa Remain Controversial

While various proposals to change the current system of adjudicating matters of federal law in American Samoa have been periodically discussed and studied, controversy remains regarding whether any changes are necessary and, if so, what options should be pursued. In the mid-1990s, various proposals to change the current system were studied by judicial committees and federal officials. Issues that were raised at that time, such as protecting American Samoan culture and traditions, resurfaced during our interviews with federal and American Samoa government officials, legal experts, and in group discussions and public comments we received. Reasons offered for changing the existing system focus primarily on the difficulties of adjudicating matters of federal law arising in American Samoa, along with the goal of providing American Samoans with more direct access to justice in their place of residence. Reasons offered against changing the current system of adjudicating matters of federal law focus largely on concerns about the impact of an increased federal presence on Samoan culture and traditions, as well as concerns regarding the impartiality of local juries.

Concerns with White-Collar Crime Led to Discussions in the Mid-1990s on Changing the System for Adjudicating Matters of Federal Law in American Samoa

The issue of changing the system for adjudicating matters of federal law in American Samoa has been raised in the past in response to a government audit and subsequent reports, which cite problems dating back to the 1980s. These reports cited problems with deteriorating financial conditions, poor financial management practices, and vulnerability to fraudulent activities in American Samoa.[41] In March 1993, the newly elected Governor of American Samoa requested assistance from the Secretary of the Interior to help investigate white-collar crime in American Samoa in response to a projected $60 million deficit uncovered by a DOI Inspector General audit.[42] As a result of this request, a team from DOJ spent 3 months assessing the problem of white-collar crime in American Samoa and completed its report in December 1994.[43] The report concluded that white-collar crime—in particular, public corruption—was prevalent in American Samoa and provided details on the difficulties with enforcing federal law in American Samoa. The report discussed three possible solutions: (1) establishing a district court in American Samoa, (2) providing the U.S. District Court of Hawaii with jurisdiction over certain matters of federal law arising in American Samoa, or (3) providing the High Court of American Samoa with federal criminal jurisdiction.

By August 1995, the U.S. Congress held hearings on the 1994 DOJ report and possible alternatives to provide for the prosecution of federal crimes arising in American Samoa. At the hearing, some American Samoa government officials opposed suggestions for changing the judicial system in the territory and concern was expressed over increased federal presence, the desire to retain self-determination regarding their judicial structure, and the need to protect and maintain the *matai* title and land tenure system in American Samoa. The American Samoa Attorney General at that time testified that his office and the Department of Public Safety had created a Joint Task Force on Public Corruption that investigated and prosecuted several white-collar offenses, including embezzlement, bribery, fraud, public corruption, forgery, and tax violations.[44]

For several months following the 1995 congressional hearings, different legislative options were studied by judicial committees within Congress and federal officials. One bill was drafted that would have given the U.S. District Court of Hawaii limited jurisdiction over federal cases arising in American Samoa. The bill proposed that one or more magistrate judges may sit in American Samoa, but district judges of the U.S. District Court of Hawaii would presumably preside over trials in Hawaii. The bill was opposed by some federal judicial officials citing an unfair burden that would be placed on the District of Hawaii, as well as on defendants, witnesses, and juries, due, in part, to the logistical difficulties in transporting them between American Samoa and Hawaii.[45] By 1996, the proposed legislation was revised to establish an Article IV court in American Samoa with full staff accompaniments and limited federal jurisdiction that would exclude cases that would put into issue the office or title of *matai* and land tenure.[46] While DOJ sent the legislation to the President of the Senate and Speaker of the House in October 1996, it was never introduced into the 104th Congress or in subsequent congressional sessions.

Concerns about Human Trafficking and Federal Grant-Related Corruption Have Heightened Law Enforcement Focus on American Samoa

While the mid-1990's legislative proposals were primarily concerned with white-collar crime in American Samoa, more recently, different types of criminal activities have emerged. Prior to 1999, FBI officials told us that allegations of criminal activity in American Samoa were investigated by agents based in the Washington, D.C. field office and, due to the distance and costs involved, very few investigations were initiated. Around mid-1999, FBI began to assign Hawaii-based agents to investigations in American Samoa in response to increasing reports of criminal activity. Then, due to growing caseload and a crime assessment, in December 2005 FBI opened a resident agency in American Samoa. According to an FBI official, other than a National Park Service fish and wildlife investigator affiliated with the National Park of American Samoa, the FBI agents were the first federal law enforcement agents to be stationed in American Samoa. FBI's increased activities over the past 8 years, and establishment of a resident agency, have targeted a growing number of crimes in American Samoa, including public corruption of high-ranking government officials, fraud against the government, civil rights violations, and human trafficking. Among the most notable was *U.S. v. Lee*, which was the largest human trafficking case ever prosecuted by DOJ, as reported in 2007.[47] This 2001 case involved about 200 Chinese and Vietnamese victims who were held in a garment factory, and in 2003, Lee was convicted in the U.S. District Court of Hawaii of involuntary servitude, conspiring to violate civil rights, extortion, and money laundering. Another federal case in 2006 resulted in guilty pleas from the prison warden and his associate for conspiring to deprive an inmate of rights, by assaulting him and causing him bodily injury.[48]

In December 2004, we found that American Samoa's failure to complete single audits,[49] federal agencies' slow reactions to this failure, and instances of theft and fraud limited accountability for 12 key federal grants supporting essential services in American Samoa.[50] We recommended, among other things, that the Secretary of the Interior coordinate with other federal agencies to designate the American Samoa government as a high-risk grantee until it completed all delinquent single audits. In June 2005, DOI designated the American Samoa government as a high-risk grantee. The American Samoa government subsequently completed all overdue audits and made efforts to comply with single audit act requirements. Later, in December 2006, we reported that insular area governments, including American Samoa, face serious economic, fiscal, and financial accountability challenges and that their abilities to strengthen their economies were constrained by their lack of diversification in industries, scarce natural resources, small domestic markets, limited infrastructure, and shortages of skilled labor.[51] Again, we cited the long-standing financial accountability problems in American Samoa, including the late submission of the reports required by the Single Audit Act, the inability to achieve unqualified ("clean") audit opinions on financial statements, and numerous material weaknesses in internal controls over financial reporting and compliance with laws and regulations governing federal grant awards.[52] We made several recommendations to the Secretary of the Interior, including increasing coordination activities with officials from other federal grant-making agencies on issues such as late single audit reports, high-risk designations, and deficiencies in financial management systems and practices. DOI agreed with our recommendations, but we have not yet assessed its progress toward implementing them.

In addition to these GAO reviews, FBI and various inspector general agents have conducted a broad investigation into federal grant-related corruption in American Samoa, which yielded guilty pleas in October 2005 from four former American Samoa government officials, including the Director of Procurement of American Samoa, the Director of the Department of Education of American Samoa, the Director of the Department of Health and Social Services for American Samoa, and the Director of the School Lunch Program for American Samoa. Additionally, recent audits and investigations by the Inspector General offices of the Departments of Homeland Security, Education, and the Interior indicate that the American Samoa government has inadequate controls and oversight over federal funds, that federal competitive bidding practices have been circumvented, and that American Samoan officials have abused federal funds for personal benefit. For example, in September 2007, officials from the U.S. Department of Education designated the American Samoa government as a high-risk grantee due to serious internal control issues raised in previous single audits, and cited a number of underlying fiscal and management problems. Due to the department's concerns about the American Samoa government's ability to properly administer and provide services with its funds, the department imposed several special conditions, including restrictions on the drawdown of grant funds. Also, the American Samoa legislature, or *Fono*, has been assisting federal agencies in their efforts to investigate public corruption and other crimes. Specifically, in early 2007, the *Fono* established a Senate Select Investigative Committee to review and investigate any unlawful, improper, wasteful, or fraudulent operations involving local and federal funds or any other misconduct involving government operations within all departments, boards, commissions, committees, and agencies of the American Samoa government. An official stated the committee reviews and investigates complaints, holds senate hearings with relevant witnesses, and can refer cases to either the American Samoa Attorney General or FBI for investigation and prosecution.

Reasons Offered for Changing the Current System Focus Principally on the Difficulties of Adjudicating Matters of Federal Law and Greater Access to Justice

As was the case in the 1990s, and was repeated in the interviews we conducted and e-mail comments we received, the reasons offered for changing the American Samoa judicial system principally stem from challenges associated with adjudicating matters of federal law arising in American Samoa and the desire to provide American Samoans with greater access to justice. Federal law enforcement officials have identified a number of issues that limit their ability to pursue matters of federal law arising in American Samoa. These include logistical challenges related to American Samoa's remote location. Proponents of changing the judicial system of American Samoa also cite reasons, such as providing more direct access to justice as in other insular areas, serving as a possible deterrent to crime, and providing a means to alleviate the shame, embarrassment, and costs associated with being taken away to be tried more than 2,000 miles from American Samoa. While the main areas of concern in the mid-1990s and in our discussions were related to criminal matters arising in American Samoa, there were also concerns regarding civil matters, such as federal debt collection, although these were not addressed in much detail.

Logistical Challenges Related to American Samoa's Remote Location

Without a federal court in American Samoa, investigators and federal prosecutors whom we interviewed said they were limited in their ability to conduct investigations and prosecute cases due to logistical obstacles related to working in such a remote location. In addition to high travel costs, and infrequent flights into and out of American Samoa, DOJ officials said they face difficulties involving effective witness preparation and difficulties communicating with agents during a small window of time each day (due to the 7-hour time difference between Washington, D.C. and American Samoa). In some cases, search warrants or wiretaps were not used by the prosecutors to the extent that they would have been if American Samoa were in closer proximity to Washington, D.C. or Honolulu, Hawaii.[53] Federal prosecutors told us that far fewer witnesses have been called to testify in front of the grand jury, given the burden of high travel costs from American Samoa. Federal prosecutors also told us that they must also rely on witness observations and summaries from federal agents stationed in American Samoa rather than meet key witnesses face to face before bringing charges or issuing subpoenas, as they would typically do. Further, according to DOJ officials, the cost related to managing these cases has limited the number of cases they are able to pursue. Federal law enforcement agents told us that a federal court located in American Samoa could bring additional investigative and prosecutorial resources so that they would be able to pursue more cases. Although some have suggested that judicial and prosecutorial resources from the judicial districts of CNMI and Guam be deployed to American Samoa, the high travel costs and logistical obstacles would not be any less, given that there are no direct flights between American Samoa and Guam or between American Samoa and CNMI. See figure 2 showing the distances between American Samoa and CNMI, Guam, Hawaii, and Washington, D.C.

More Direct Access to Federal Court and Parity with Other Insular Areas

Another key reason offered for changing the system for adjudicating matters of federal law in American Samoa is that a federal court would provide residents with more direct access to justice and the ability to pursue cases in the federal court system. Currently, the ability to adjudicate federal cases exists only in very limited cases through the High Court, at a significant cost of time and money to travel to U.S. District Courts in Hawaii or Washington, D.C.; or not at all, in the case of some civil matters and bankruptcy. Proponents state that the establishment of a federal court would provide American Samoa parity with other insular areas, such as CNMI, Guam, and USVI, which have federal courts. Further, a legal expert said that a federal court in American Samoa would provide the community with an opportunity to see first hand how parties can come together to resolve their differences with regard to federal matters. For example, some have asserted that if public corruption trials were held in American Samoa, they would act as a deterrent to others contemplating fraudulent behavior; increase accountability with regard to government spending; and provide satisfaction in witnessing wrong doers brought to justice. Some stated in the February 2006 public hearing held by the *Fono*[54]and in e-mail comments we received that they have felt shame and embarrassment when defendants are taken to distant courts and in our group discussions, it was stated that American Samoa is perceived by others as unable to render justice to its own residents. Further, some officials of American Samoa have noted the significant costs that defendants' families must bear in traveling great distances to provide support during trials. This burden is exacerbated by the comparatively low family incomes in American Samoa, which, as stated earlier, are less than half of the U.S. median household income, according to 2000 Census Bureau data.

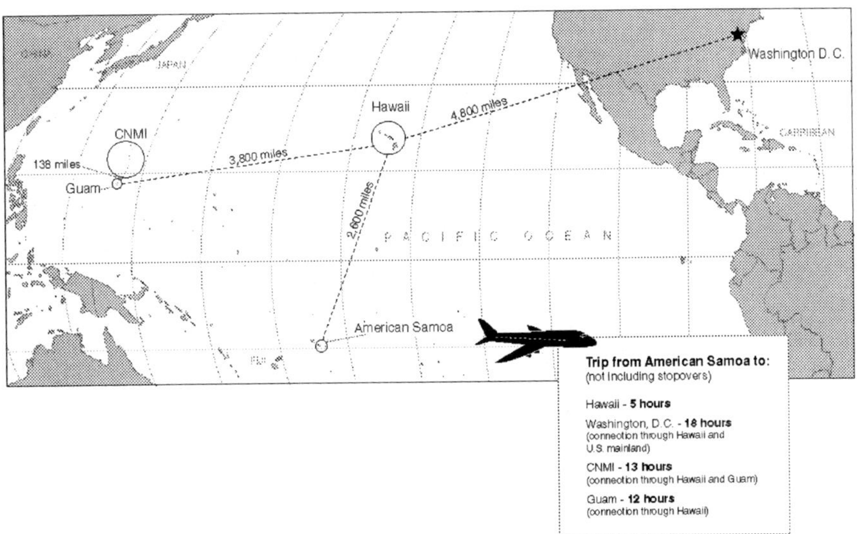

Source: GAO (art, analysis), MapResources (map).

Figure 2. Map Showing Distances and Flying Times between American Samoa and CNMI, Guam, Hawaii, andWashington, D.C.

Finally, some people we met with stated that the current system of holding federal criminal trials outside of American Samoa subjects defendants to possible prejudices by jurors in other locations. They cited the relative unfamiliarity of the judges and jurors in Washington, D.C. or Honolulu, Hawaii regarding American Samoa cultural and political issues and suggested that American Samoans would receive a fairer trial in American Samoa than in these locations. This issue had also been discussed in the mid-1990s. For example, in his testimony during August 1995 congressional hearings, the then-Governor of American Samoa stated that the people of American Samoa have the ability to deliver just verdicts based on the evidence presented. He noted that for almost 20 years prior, the trial division of the High Court had successfully conducted six-person jury trials as evidence that American Samoan customs and family loyalties had not prevented effective law enforcement.[55]

Comments from Group Discussions and E-mail Responses Reflect Some of the Same Reasons Offered for Changing the Current System

Views in support of changing the current system were also reflected in some comments made during the group discussions we held in American Samoa and in some of the e-mail responses we received. Some members of the public expressed discontent over the significant costs associated with American Samoan defendants and their families having to travel to Hawaii or Washington, D.C. for court matters and they expressed the importance of having a jury of their peers deciding their cases. Other members of the public and a local community group expressed their belief that a federal court in American Samoa may act as a deterrent for the abuse of federal funds and public corruption, and provide opportunities for American Samoans to pursue federal legal matters, such as bankruptcy. While there was no consensus opinion, certain members of the local bar association mentioned that having a federal court could be beneficial for economic development, by attracting qualified attorneys and court staff to American Samoa. Additionally, one member stated that a federal court may lighten the workload and reduce the backlog of the High Court by taking over its federal maritime and admiralty matters.

Reasons Offered against Changing the Current Judicial System Focus Principally on Preserving the Culture and Traditions of American Samoa and Concerns about Juries

One of the key reasons offered against changing the current judicial system is the concern that a federal court would impinge upon Samoan culture and traditions. The most frequent concerns raised were related issues— that the system of *matai* chiefs and the land tenure system could be jeopardized. In raising these issues, some cited the deeds of cession which specify that the United States would preserve the rights and property of the Samoan people. Further, some law enforcement officials we met with also opposed a change to the current system for prosecuting federal cases arising in American Samoa because they were concerned that, given the close familial ties in American Samoa, it would be difficult to obtain convictions from local jurors.

Preservation of Local Culture and Traditions

During the February 2006 *Fono* hearings,[56] in e-mail comments we received, and in statements by American Samoa government officials we interviewed, concerns were voiced that the establishment of a federal court in American Samoa could jeopardize the *matai* and land tenure system of American Samoa. As noted above, *matai* hold positions of authority in the community; for example, only *matai* may serve as senators in the American Samoa legislature, and *matai* control the use and development of the communal lands and allocate housing to their extended family members. The land tenure system of American Samoa is such that the majority of the land in American Samoa is communally owned, and the sale or exchange of communally owned land is prohibited without the consent of the Governor. Also prohibited is the sale or exchange of communally owned and individually owned property to people with less than one-half Samoan blood.[57] American Samoa government officials assert that the land tenure system fosters the strong familial and community ties that are the backbone of Samoan culture and that limits on the transfer of land are important to preserve the lands of American Samoa for Samoans and protect the Samoan culture.

Currently, cases regarding *matai* titles and land issues, such as disputes over the rightful successor to a *matai* or land use or improvements, are heard by the land and titles division of the High Court of American Samoa. This division is composed of the Chief Justice and Associate Justice, as well as associate judges, who are appointed based on their knowledge of Samoan culture and tradition. Pursuant to the federalist structure of the U.S. judiciary, if a federal court were established in American Samoa most cases arising under local law, such as *matai* and land disputes, would likely continue to be heard by the local court. However, some American Samoa officials stated that they are concerned that if a federal court were established in American Samoa, federal judges, without the requisite knowledge of Samoan culture and tradition, would hear land and title cases. They stated that they would like to keep *matai* title and land tenure issues within the jurisdiction of the High Court.

Another concern that was raised by government officials and residents of American Samoa is that the presence of a federal court in American Samoa may generate constitutional challenges to the *matai* and land tenure system. Though such challenges may be brought in existing venues, some voiced concerns that the establishment of a federal court in American Samoa may make such challenges less costly and perhaps more likely.

In general, many residents of American Samoa said they value their culture and traditions and think that the *matai* and land tenure systems in American Samoa are critical components of the *fa'a Samoa*. The following quote from the Secretary of Samoan Affairs summarizes the position we heard from many during our visit:

> To this day, our native land tenure system remains at the very core of our existence: our culture, our heritage and our way of life. Without our native land tenure system, our matai or chieftain system will fade over time—along with our language, our customs and our culture....we, as a people, have an overriding desire to keep the fabric of our society (i.e., our Samoan culture) intact. No other U.S. state or territory enjoys the total and complete preservation of its people's culture as American Samoa. I fear that the imposition of a federal court system in American Samoa may have a destructive impact on our culture.[58]

Concerns about Juries

Some have raised concerns regarding the establishment of a federal jury system, given the potentially small pool of U.S. citizens in American Samoa and the extended family ties among American Samoans. Federal law provides that federal jurors must be U.S. citizens. [59] As discussed earlier, American Samoans are U.S. nationals, not U.S. citizens, although they may apply and become U.S. citizens. Neither the U.S. Census Bureau nor the American Samoa Department of Commerce provides data on the number of U.S. citizens in American Samoa. Thus, the proportion of the American Samoa adult population who are U.S. citizens is unknown. If the number of U.S. citizens is fairly small, then the pool from which to select federal jurors would be fairly small without a statutory change. In addition, law enforcement officials have speculated that extended family ties in American Samoa may limit the government's ability to successfully prosecute cases. Specifically, they raised the issue of jury nullification—the rendering of a not guilty verdict even though the jury believes that the defendant committed the offense—as a potential problem that may occur if jury trials were held in American Samoa, due to the influence of familial ties or other societal pressures on jurors. Federal law enforcement officials we met with added that some witnesses involved in testifying against others in previous federal criminal cases have relocated outside of American Samoa and have lost their jobs and housing as a result of their participation in cases. These officials stated that they believe that similar societal pressures will be imposed on jurors if trials were held in American Samoa. These officials concluded that the current system of federal criminal trials taking place away from American Samoa is the best way to get unbiased juries.[60]

Comments from Group Discussions and E-mail Responses Reflect Some of the Same Reasons Offered against Changing the Current System

Views expressing opposition to changing the current system were also reflected in some comments we received from the group discussions we held in American Samoa and from e-mail responses. Some members of the public expressed concerns over an increased federal presence in American Samoa and the potential legal challenges which could be brought regarding the land tenure system and *matai* title traditions. Further, some expressed concerns about non-Samoans filing discrimination lawsuits over their inability to own land. Some stated that the current system operates well and they did not see a need for change. Others expressed opposition to a federal court in American Samoa due to their concerns about impartial jurors. They stated that if a federal court were established in American Samoa, jurors may not be able to be impartial because of the close relations through family, culture, church, government, or business. Finally, others expressed concerns about the U.S. government pushing and imposing its will on American Samoa, and their belief that changes to the current system should come not from the federal government but from American Samoans themselves.

Scenarios for Establishing a Federal Court in American Samoa or Expanding the Federal Jurisdiction of the High Court of American Samoa Have Varied Support and Unresolved Issues

Based on our review of legislative proposals considered during the mid-1990s testimonies and reports and through discussions with legal experts and American Samoa and federal government officials, we identified three potential proposals, or scenarios, if a change to the judicial system of American Samoa were to be made. These scenarios are (1) establishing an Article IV district court in American Samoa, (2) establishing a district court in American Samoa that would be a division of the District of Hawaii, or (3) expanding the federal jurisdiction of the High Court of American Samoa. Each scenario would require a statutory change and present unique operational issues to be addressed. To the extent possible, we cited written documents and knowledgeable sources in the discussion of these issues. See appendix I for detailed information on our scope and methodology.

Three Scenarios Present Different Structures and Operational Issues to Be Resolved

Based on our review of past legislative proposals, testimonies, and reports, and through discussions with legal experts and American Samoa and federal government officials, we identified three potential scenarios for establishing a federal court in American Samoa or expanding the federal jurisdiction of the High Court of American Samoa:

(1) establishing an Article IV district court in American Samoa,
(2) establishing a district court in American Samoa that would be a division of the District of Hawaii, or
(3) expanding the federal jurisdiction of the High Court of American Samoa.

Table 5. Description of Scenarios for Establishing a Federal Court in American Samoa or Expanding the Federal Jurisdiction of the High Court of American Samoa

	Scenario 1	Scenario 2	Scenario 3
Structure	Federal court modeled on other federal courts in U.S. territories.	District court in American Samoa that is a division of the District of Hawaii.	Unique arrange-ment granting the High Court federal criminal jurisdiction as well as expanded federal civil jurisdiction.
Judge and court staff	Article IV judge in American Samoa with court clerk and support staff.	Article IV or Article III judge in American Samoa with court clerk and support staff.	High Court Justi-ces would hear additional federal matters.
	Judge appointed by President with advice and consent of the Senate.	Judge appointed by President with advice and consent of the Senate.	Additional judge may be required, who may be appointed by the Secretary of the Interior or, as with other federal judges, by the President, with advice and cons-ent of the Senate.
U.S. Attorney	One resident U.S. Attorney with three staff attorn-eys and support staff.	Share U.S. Attorn-ey with District of Hawaii and staff a satellite office with one Assistant U.S. Attorney, three staff attorneys, and support staff.	May use a feder-al prosecutor and/or local Atto-rney General.
Defender Services	Shared federal Public defender with District of Hawaii[a] (using staff based in Hawaii) and/or CJA Panel.[b]	Shared federal Public defender with District of Hawaii[a] (using staff based in Hawaii) and/or CJA Panel.[b]	Under current law, federal def-ender services are not provided unless within a judicial district. May be able to use a local public defender.

Table 5. (Continued)

	Scenario 1	Scenario 2	Scenario 3
U.S. Marshals Service	One U.S. Marshal, one chief deputy, one judicial sec-urity inspector, two deputy marshals, and one adminis-trative staff.	Share U.S. Marshal with Hawaii and staff a satellite off-ice with supervisory deputy marshal, two deputy mars-hals, and one admi-nistrative staff.	Federal detention and security req-uirements may not apply. May be able to use a local marshal or law enforcement staff.
Probation and Pretrial Services	One chief proba-tion officer, one probation officer and one administr-ative staff in Ame-rican Samoa with shared staff in District of Hawaii for additional support.	One chief probati-on officer, one pro-bation officer and one administrative staff in American Samoa with shared staff in District of Hawaii for additional support.	Under current law, federal Probation and Pretrial servi-ces are not provi-ded unless within a judicial district.
Facilities	New courthouse facility would be needed that can house judge, court staff, U.S. Attorney staff, U.S. Marshal staff, and holding facility. Unclear whether new fede-ral dete-ntion center would be needed or whether a portion of the existing local prison could be upgraded.	New courthouse facility would be needed that can house judge, court staff, U.S. Attorney staff, U.S. Marshal staff, and holding facility. Unclear whether new federal deten-tion center would be needed or whet-her a portion of the existing local prison could be upgraded.	Federal court req-uirements may not apply. May be able to use exis-ting High Court or District Court fac-ilities. Unclear whether a new prison would be needed or whether a portion of the existing prison could be upgraded.
Jurisdiction	May be jurisdi-ction of district court and bankrup-tcy court, or may be more limited.	May be jurisdiction of district court and bankruptcy court, or may be more limited.	Limited jurisd-iction, which may grow over time.
Appeals	Appeals to U.S. Court of Appeals for the Ninth Circuit.	Same as District of Hawaii (appeals to U.S. Court of Appeals for the Ninth Circuit).	It is unclear whe-ther and to which tribunal High Co-urt decisions wou-ld be appealed.

Source: GAO analysis of relevant federal laws.

[a] According to Federal Public Defender officials, it is unlikely that a court in American Samoa would reach the minimum 200 appointments per year required to appoint a Federal Public Defender in American Samoa.

[b] U.S. district courts, with the approval of the judicial council of the circuit, must have a plan for furnishing representation for any person financially unable to obtain adequate representation. Under this plan, a judge can appoint counsel from a federal defender organization authorized by the court or a panel of attorneys designated or approved by the court—called a Criminal Justice Act (CJA) panel—to furnish legal representation for those defendants who are financially unable to obtain counsel. 18 U.S.C. § 3006A. Where a federal defender organization is established, the CJA provides that panel attorneys be appointed in a substantial proportion of the cases (defined by guidelines as approximately 25 percent of the appointments annually in a district).

These scenarios are similar to those discussed in the 1990s, and are described in table 5. Each scenario would require a statutory change and each presents unique operational issues that would need to be resolved prior to implementation. Some issues to be resolved include determining:

(1) what jurisdiction would be granted to the court;
(2) what type of courthouse facility and detention arrangements would be needed and to what standards, including security standards; and
(3) what jury eligibility requirements would apply.

Scenario 1. Establishing an Article IV District Court in American Samoa

The original structure of this scenario came from draft legislation submitted by DOJ to the Speaker of the U.S. House of Representatives and the President of the U.S. Senate in October 1996, which proposed the creation of a new federal court in American Samoa.[61] The legislation specified that the court would have limited jurisdiction that would exclude matters pertaining to *matai* title and land tenure issues. Under this scenario, federal law would authorize a federal court structure that most closely resembled federal courts in CNMI, Guam, and USVI. It would include an Article IV district court with a district judge, court clerk, and support staff. Below is a description of the key issues under this scenario.

Jurisdiction: The statute creating the Article IV district court would specify the court's jurisdiction. It could be limited to criminal cases only, or may or may not include bankruptcy, federal question, and diversity jurisdiction. American Samoa officials and others whom we interviewed were divided on whether the law establishing a district court in American Samoa should explicitly exclude *matai* and land tenure issues from the court's jurisdiction. Another possibility is that, as in other insular area federal courts, the federal jurisdiction of the court could grow over time. For example, while the District Court of Guam began with jurisdiction over cases arising under federal law in 1950, subsequent federal laws expanded its jurisdiction to include that of a district court of the United States, including diversity jurisdiction, and that of a bankruptcy court.

Appeals process: The process for appealing decisions would be the same as in other Article IV district courts. Appeals would first go to the U.S. Court of Appeals for the Ninth Circuit and then to the U.S. Supreme Court.

Judges: The judge would be appointed in the same manner as federal judges for the other insular areas, who are appointed by the President, with the advice and consent of the Senate, for 10-year terms.

Associated Executive and Judicial Branch staff: Probation and Pretrial services staff, U.S. Attorney and staff, and U.S. Marshals staff would establish stand-alone offices. Defender services could be provided, at least initially, through the Federal Public Defender Organization personnel based in the District of Hawaii and/or Criminal Justice Act (CJA) panel attorneys.[62] CJA panel attorneys are designated or approved by the court to furnish legal representation for those defendants who are financially unable to obtain counsel.[63]

Physical facilities: Under this scenario, a new courthouse facility would need to be built to provide the courtroom, judge's chambers, office space for federal court staff, and a holding area for detaining defendants during trials. It is not clear if a detention facility for detaining defendants pretrial and presentencing would need to be built or if a portion of the existing local prison could be upgraded to meet federal standards. According to the U.S. Marshals Service, the current local prison in American Samoa does not meet federal detention standards.

Operational issues: Several judicial officials and experts we met with stated that this scenario is the most straightforward option because it would be modeled after the federal courts in other insular areas, which would place residents of American Samoa in a position that is equitable with residents of the other insular areas. Other judicial officials we met with stated, however, that this is potentially the most costly scenario of the three, given the relatively small caseload expected. However, the Pacific Islands Committee[64] stated in its 1995 Supplemental Report that new federal courts historically have drawn business as soon as they open their doors, and it is likely that growth in the court caseload would result.[65]

Scenario 2. Establishing a District Court in American Samoa That Would Be a Division of the District of Hawaii

This scenario would create a new division of American Samoa within the District of Hawaii.[66] There are potentially several arrangements which could be devised to handle court matters. Since the U.S. District Court of Hawaii is an Article III court, a judge assigned to a Division of American Samoa would also presumably be an Article III judge, which would differ from the Article IV courts in CNMI, Guam, and USVI. Another possibility would be to assign an Article IV judge to American Samoa. Regardless of the arrangement, a clerk of the court and support staff would be needed in American Samoa to handle the work of the court.

Jurisdiction: As with scenario 1, the statute creating the division in the District of Hawaii would specify the court's jurisdiction. It could be limited to criminal cases only, or may or may not include bankruptcy, federal question, and diversity jurisdiction.

Appeals process: The process for appealing decisions would be the same as the District of Hawaii, to the U.S. Court of Appeals for the Ninth Circuit and then to the U.S. Supreme Court.

Judges: An Article III or Article IV judge would be appointed by the President, with the advice and consent of the Senate, and serve either a life term with good behavior (Article III) or a 10-year term (Article IV) as is true in Guam, CNMI, and USVI.

Associated Executive and Judicial Branch staff: Probation and Pretrial services, U.S. Attorney, and U.S. Marshals could provide the minimum staff required in American Samoa and share support functions with their offices in the District of Hawaii. Defender services could be provided, at least initially, through Federal Public Defender Organization personnel based in the U.S. District Court of Hawaii and/or CJA panel attorneys.

Physical facilities: As with scenario 1, a new courthouse facility would need to be built to provide the courtroom, judge's chambers, office space for federal court staff, and a holding area for detaining defendants during trials.

Also, similar to scenario 1, it is unclear whether a new detention facility would need to be built or if a portion of the existing local prison could be upgraded to meet federal standards.

Operational issues: Some federal and judicial officials we interviewed told us that this scenario may be less costly than scenario 1 because as a division of the District of Hawaii, some administrative functions and resources may be able to be shared with Hawaii. Other federal and judicial officials told us that costs for staff to travel between American Samoa and Hawaii and additional supervisory staff which may be needed in Hawaii may make scenario 2 just as costly, or possibly more costly than scenario 1. Although this scenario would allow for trials to be held in American Samoa, there may be issues to be resolved concerning the status of any judges that would serve in the court and the degree to which resources would be shared with the U.S. District Court of Hawaii. For example, some judicial officials have raised questions of equity about the possibility of Article IV judges being assigned to federal courts in CNMI, Guam, and USVI while an Article III judge was assigned to the federal court in American Samoa.

Scenario 3. Expanding the Federal Jurisdiction of the High Court of American Samoa

This scenario would expand the federal jurisdiction of the High Court of American Samoa rather than establish a new federal court. This would be a unique structure, as local courts typically do not exercise federal criminal jurisdiction. As a result, a number of unresolved issues associated with this scenario would have to be resolved should this scenario be pursued.

Jurisdiction: The jurisdiction of the High Court would be expanded to include additional federal matters, such as federal criminal jurisdiction. This would be a unique structure, as local courts generally do not exercise federal criminal jurisdiction. While there is a history of federal courts in insular areas with jurisdiction over local offenses, there has never been the reverse—a local court with jurisdiction over both local and federal offenses.

Appeals process: The appellate process for federal matters under such a scenario is unclear. The current process for the limited federal cases handled by the High Court has five levels of appellate review: (1) to the Appellate Division of the High Court, (2) to the Secretary of the Interior, (3) to the U.S. District Court for the District of Columbia, (4) to the U.S. Court of Appeals for the District of Columbia Circuit, and (5) to the U.S. Supreme Court. Whether the appeals process would match that of the federal courts in CNMI, Guam, and USVI would have to be determined.

Judges: The Chief Justice of the High Court stated that the High Court may need an additional judge to handle the increased caseload. Alternatively, in our discussions, Pacific Island Committee members with whom we met suggested that the Secretary of the Interior or the Chief Judge of the Ninth Circuit could designate active and senior district judges within the Ninth Circuit to handle any court workload in American Samoa. They point out that they designated judges from the Ninth Circuit to the District of Guam for over 2 years, when there was an extended judge vacancy. Further, the Ninth Circuit has designated local judges to handle federal matters, when necessary. For example, the judges from the Districts of CNMI and Guam routinely use local Superior Court or Supreme Court judges to handle federal court matters and trials, in cases when they must recuse themselves from a court matter or in the case of a planned or emergency absence.

However, Pacific Island Committee members with whom we met stated that presumably federal judges would only handle federal court matters. It was unclear whether High Court justices would handle federal and local court matters and what implications might arise from such a structure.

Associated Executive and Judicial Branch staff: It is unclear whether Probation and Pretrial services, U.S. Attorneys, and U.S. Marshals would be established, since these staff are only provided to a district court. Similarly, the authority under the CJA to authorize a federal defender organization to provide representation or to compensate panel attorneys is vested in the district court. The Department of Justice would need to determine whether it would establish a federal prosecutor position in American Samoa to prosecute certain federal cases in the High Court. There are local Public Defender and Attorney General Offices in American Samoa and the extent to which they could assist with cases is unknown. According to the Chief Justice of the High Court, it is unlikely that the existing probation and pretrial or court security staff would be able to handle an increased workload. Currently the High Court has three probation officers who work part-time as translators for the court, and two marshals, one for each of the High Court's two courtrooms.

Physical facilities: The extent to which federal detention and courtroom security requirements would apply is uncertain. Until this issue is resolved, activities could possibly continue in existing courthouse and detention facilities. However, the High Court justices and clerk said that current courtroom facilities are already used to capacity without the added caseload that federal jurisdiction could bring.

Operational issues: This scenario may be the lowest-cost scenario and may alleviate concerns about the threat to the *matai* and land tenure systems. It is potentially the lowest-cost scenario because some of the existing court facilities and staff may be used. Some leaders within the American Samoa government believe this is the best option and supporters of this scenario note that the High Court has a history of respecting American Samoa traditions and so they have fewer concerns that issues of *matai* titles and land tenure would be in jeopardy.

At the same time, as it is unprecedented to give federal criminal jurisdiction to a local court, this scenario could face the most challenges of the three, according to federal judges and other judicial officials. Legal experts with whom we met told us that, because this is a unique arrangement, the High Court and U.S. judiciary may be faced with having to constantly solve unique problems and develop solutions on a regular basis. For example, judicial officials stated that the High Court Justices would have to be cognizant of their roles and responsibilities when shifting from the duties of a local High Court Justice to the duties of a federal judge. A judicial official also noted that the High Court justices may have to become familiar with federal sentencing guidelines, which require a considerable amount of training. In the August 1995 hearing, the DOJ Deputy Assistant Attorney General stated that vesting federal jurisdiction in the High Court runs counter to well-established legislative policy that district courts should have exclusive jurisdiction over certain types of proceedings to which the United States is a party. For example, federal law states that U.S. district courts have exclusive jurisdiction over all offenses against the criminal laws of the United States[67] and with respect to the collection of debts owed to the United States, provides for an exclusive debt collection procedure in the courts created by Congress.[68] Similarly, federal regulatory statutes often provide for enforcement and judicial review in the federal courts.

Another issue to be resolved is the appointment process for justices of the High Court. While none of the judicial officials with whom we met had concerns about the independence of the current justices, some expressed concerns about the differences in the way judges are appointed—while federal judges are generally appointed by the President, the justices in American Samoa are appointed by the Secretary of the Interior. As such, they suggested that the justices in American Samoa may not be subject to the same vetting process and protected by the same constitutional and statutory provisions—such as salary guarantees—as are district judges.

POTENTIAL COST ELEMENTS SUBJECT TO CONSIDERABLE UNCERTAINTIES

The potential cost elements for establishing a federal court in American Samoa include agency rental costs, personnel costs, and operational costs; most of which would be funded by congressional appropriations. We collected likely cost elements, to the extent possible, for scenario 1 and 2 from the various federal agencies that would be involved in establishing a federal court in American Samoa. We did not collect cost data for scenario 3 because of its unique judicial arrangement and because there was no comparable existing federal court structure upon which to estimate costs. For scenario 1 and 2, AOUSC officials told us that a new courthouse would need to be built. GSA officials told us that court construction and agency rental costs would be comparatively high—about $80 to $90 per square foot for a new courthouse, compared to typical federal government rental charges for office space in American Samoa of around $45 to $50 per square foot in 2007. Funding sources for the judiciary and DOJ derive primarily from direct congressional appropriations and funding for a federal courthouse in American Samoa would likely be funded similarly. We found the data for scenarios 1 and 2 sufficiently reliable to provide rough estimates of the possible future costs for these scenarios for establishing a federal court in American Samoa, with limitations as noted.

Data Limitations and Assumptions

Because the three court scenarios presented are hypothetical, and the exact details of the jurisdiction, staffing, and physical facilities would have to be determined when, and if, a specific scenario were adopted, the estimated costs cannot be aggregated to obtain a precise estimate of the total costs for the scenarios. Rather, the cost data should be viewed as general approximations of the types and magnitude of costs that could be incurred. Recognizing this uncertainty, we collected likely cost elements for each scenario, to the extent possible, from federal agencies that would be involved in establishing a federal court in American Samoa—GSA for construction and rental costs, AOUSC for judicial branch costs, and EOUSA and USMS for executive branch costs.

We collected cost data for scenarios 1 and 2. According to AOUSC, under each of these scenarios a new courthouse would need to be built. We did not estimate costs for bankruptcy courts for either scenario, since, if the district court were to hear bankruptcy cases, it is likely that the district court judge would hear both federal matters and bankruptcy cases, similar to other district judges in CNMI, Guam, and USVI. We did not collect cost data for scenario 3 because, as stated earlier, it would be a unique judicial arrangement and there is no comparable existing federal court structure upon which to estimate costs. The cost data presented cannot be used for budget purposes and an analysis of cost effectiveness would be of limited value given that the data are fragmented. The controversy surrounding whether and how to create a venue for adjudicating matters of federal law in American Samoa is not principally focused on an analysis of cost effectiveness, but other policy considerations, such as equity, justice, and cultural preservation. Thus, policy considerations, other than cost effectiveness, are more likely to be the basis for deciding whether and how to establish a court with federal jurisdiction in American Samoa. For a detailed description of the scope and methodology, including the caveats and limitations of the cost data, see appendix I.

Court Construction and Agency Rental Costs Would be Comparatively High

Due to limitations on existing buildings and potential land restrictions—about 90 percent of American Samoan land is communally owned—GSA officials told us that a new courthouse in American Samoa would likely use a build-to-suit lease construction arrangement rather than government-owned construction and that construction and consequent rental costs would be comparatively high. GSA provided initial construction and rental costs for the hypothetical courthouse in American Samoa, based on a floor plan submitted for a proposed new one-judge courthouse in CNMI. According to GSA officials, there are no buildings in American Samoa suitable for use as a federal courthouse. Further, officials from the High Court of American Samoa told us that its two-courtroom High Court building and its one-courtroom local district court building are frequently used to capacity.

Under build-to-lease construction, the government contracts with a private developer to build the courthouse and, in this case, GSA leases the completed building based on the amortization of a 20-year construction loan. GSA would then rent portions of the building to the tenant federal agencies, such as AOUSC, EOUSA, and USMS. GSA officials gave very preliminary rent estimates of $80 to $90 per square foot,[69] based on requirements similar to an existing build-to-suit lease prospectus for a new courthouse in CNMI.[70] Further, GSA officials told us that federal agencies would be responsible for up-front payments for the particular courthouse governmental features, such as holding cells, and blast protection for security.[71] GSA officials indicate that the accuracy of the initial American Samoa court construction may vary by as much as -20 to +80 percent, thereby influencing rental costs. The GSA Assistant Regional Administrator for Region IX Pacific Rim stated that there are many factors that could affect construction costs and, therefore, the tenant agencies' rental costs. For example, any cost increases associated with the condition of an unknown site or escalation in construction costs beyond what has been anticipated will have a direct and proportional impact on the rental costs, as well as the up-front costs that agencies may be required to pay.

Preliminary rental costs of $80 to $90 per square foot for a new courthouse with specialized building requirements would exceed typical federal government rental charges for offices in American Samoa at the prevailing market rates of $45 to $50 per rentable square foot in 2007.

Judicial Branch Costs Include Judges, Court Staff, and Federal Defender

For scenarios 1 and 2, AOUSC officials provided information related to four types of costs:

(1) district court costs,
(2) probation and pretrial services costs, and
(3) federal defender office costs.

Scenario 1 Costs

District court costs: For yearly district court costs under scenario 1, AOUSC provided us with district court cost estimates of about $1.5 million for personnel costs, including the costs of one district court judge and the full-time equivalent salaries of 2 law clerks and 1 secretary, 11 district clerk's office staff, 1 pro se law clerk,[72] 1 court reporter, and recruitment and training costs.[73] Operational costs were estimated at $0.1 million, which includes judge's law books, stationery, forms, new case assignment and jury management systems, travel, postage and delivery charges, and consumables for both the first year and recurring years. Information technology and other equipment costs were estimated at $0.1 million. Space and facilities costs ranged between $2.6 million to $2.9 million and include necessary alterations and renovations, signage, furnishings, furniture, and estimated GSA rental costs.[74]

Probation and pretrial services costs: For the yearly cost of probation and pretrial services, AOUSC provided us with personnel and benefits costs estimated at $0.3 million, which includes the full-time equivalent salaries of one Chief Probation Officer, one probation officer, and one administrative support staff. Operational costs were estimated at $0.1 million, including travel, training, transportation, postage, printing, maintenance, drug dependent offender testing and aftercare, pretrial drug testing, mental health treatment services, monitoring services, DNA testing, notices/advertising, contractual services, supplies, awards, firearms, and protective equipment. Information technology and other equipment costs were estimated at about $16,000 (i.e., equipment, maintenance, purchase of copy equipment, computer training, phone communications, supplies, computers, phones, data communications equipment, printers, scanner, and computer software).[75] Space and facilities costs were estimated at $0.4 million to $0.5 million, which includes furniture and fixture purchases, as well as GSA rental costs.[76]

Federal Defender costs: AOUSC officials did not estimate costs for a Federal Defender's office, since it is unlikely that the hypothetical court in American Samoa would, at least initially, reach the minimum 200 appointments per year required to authorize a Federal Defender Organization or the number of cases that would warrant the creation of a Federal Public Defender Organization headquartered in the District of Hawaii. The court in American Samoa, as an adjacent district, might be able to share the Federal Public Defender Organization staff based in Hawaii, or the court could rely solely on a CJA panel of attorneys.[77] The costs to the Federal Public Defender Organization in Hawaii and the costs of reimbursing CJA attorneys would vary based on the caseload of the court.

Scenario 2 Costs

District Court costs: According to AOUSC, the estimated district court costs for scenario 2 could be similar to the estimated costs for scenario 1. AOUSC officials indicated that there may not be a need for a clerk, financial/procurement officer, jury clerk, or information technology specialist in American Samoa under scenario 2, as those functions may be handled out of the District of Hawaii office, leading to some possible reductions in personnel salaries. However, some judicial officials stated that any decrease in staff costs for this scenario may be offset by increased costs for travel between Hawaii and American Samoa. GSA rental costs would be comparable to scenario 1.

Probation and pretrial services costs: Probation and Pretrial Services officials did not provide any cost differences between scenarios 1 and 2.

Federal Defender costs: Either the Office of the Federal Public Defender in Hawaii or a CJA panel may provide defender services in American Samoaunder both situations, thereby also not leading to any significant change in cost estimates between scenarios 1 and 2.

Executive Branch Costs Include Federal Prosecution and Security Costs

For the Department of Justice, an EOUSA official provided U.S. Attorney's Office cost estimates and a USMS official provided security cost estimates for both scenario 1 and scenario 2.

U.S. Attorney's Office Costs

Scenario 1 costs: EOUSA officials calculated the cost of a U.S. Attorney's office based on a partial first year and a complete second year. Modular personnel costs are $0.6 million for the first year and $1.0 million for the second year, which includes one U.S. Attorney, three attorneys, and two support staff. Operational costs ranged from $0.5 million to $0.9 million, including travel and transportation, utilities, advisory and assistance services, printing and reproduction, and supplies and materials.[78] Information technology costs were estimated at $0.1 million for equipment and the operation and maintenance of equipment. Space and facilities costs range between $1.3 million and $1.4 million and include the operation and maintenance of facilities and rent to GSA[79] and others.

Scenario 2 costs: EOUSA officials calculated U.S. Attorney's office personnel costs for a partial first year and a complete second year. Modular personnel costs rose from $0.6 million in the first year to $1.0 million throughout the second year, which includes four attorneys and two support staff. Operational costs remain consistent at $0.2 million for both the first and second years, reflecting travel and transportation, litigation costs, supplies, and other miscellaneous costs. Information technology and equipment costs were estimated to be approximately $0.1 million for both years. Yearly rental rates may also be comparable in the initial years. Personnel and operations costs for scenario 2 were estimated to be less than for scenario 1 because scenario 2 does not include a separate U.S. Attorney for American Samoa. Rather, the costs for scenario 2 are based on the estimated costs and personnel the U.S. Attorney for the District of Hawaii would need to support cases that arise in American Samoa.

U.S. Marshals Service Costs

Scenario 1 costs: USMS officials estimated that personnel costs were $0.8 million, based on fiscal year 2008 salaries, benefits, and law enforcement availability pay for all supervisory (one U.S. Marshal, one Chief Deputy, one Judicial Security Inspector) and nonsupervisory (two Deputy Marshals and one administrative) personnel that would be needed.[80] Operational costs were estimated to be $0.8 million based on fiscal year 2008 standard, nonpersonnel costs for district operational and administrative positions (including vehicles, weapons, protective gear, communications equipment, and operational travel costs), and $0.7 million for defendant transport (including guard wages, airfare, per diem meals, and lodging).[81] Information technology and equipment costs were estimated at $0.6 million for the installation of a computer network and telephone system to all USMS offices, and $0.2 million for yearly service on the wide-area network to American Samoa.[82] Space and facilities costs were estimated between $1.1 million and $1.3 million for rent,[83] plus variable defendant detention facility housing costs.[84]

Scenario 2 costs: With regard to scenario 2, USMS officials estimated that yearly personnel costs would be $0.5 million. Since a U.S. Marshal, Chief

Deputy, and Judicial Security Officer would be shared with the USMS in Hawaii and not be located in American Samoa, personnel costs for this scenario are estimated to be approximately $0.4 million less than scenario 1. Operational costs (reflecting the standard, nonpersonnel costs for operational and administrative positions) under scenario 2 were estimated to be $0.5 million, or about $0.3 million less than scenario 1. The operational cost differential between the two scenarios with respect to prisoner transport is unclear.[85] While the USMS did not specifically address information technology costs and other equipment costs with respect to scenario 2, the same types of costs in scenario 1 would be involved if a computer network and telephone system would need to be established. With respect to space and facilities, if the USMS were housed in the same court building as used for scenario 1, rental costs should be comparable (between $1.1 million and $1.3 million.) If, however, under scenario 2, the USMS were housed in an office building rather than a courthouse, then the resulting cost may be lower than scenario 1. Additionally, to the extent that defendants are detained in the same facilities as in scenario 1 (e.g., the Bureau of Prisons detention facility in Hawaii), detention facility costs should be comparable.

Potential Funding Sources Associated with Implementing the Different Scenarios

Funding for the federal judiciary and DOJ agencies derives primarily from direct congressional appropriations to each agency and funding for a federal court in American Samoa would likely be funded similarly. In fiscal year 2006, about 94 percent of the total court salary and expense obligations were obtained through direct judiciary funding. The remaining 6 percent was obtained through offsetting collections, such as fees. In that same year, about 95 percent of the total Probation and Pretrial Services obligations were obtained through direct congressional appropriations.

With regard to DOJ, in fiscal year 2006, 96 percent of the U.S. Attorneys' obligations to support district court activities were obtained through direct congressional appropriations and the remaining 4 percent were obtained through other sources, such as asset forfeitures. In fiscal year 2008, USMS used direct congressional appropriations to cover the expenses for staff hiring, payroll, relocation, personnel infrastructure, rent, and utilities. The Office of the Federal Detention Trustee funds 100 percent of prisoner detention, meals, medical care, and transportation. AOUSC funds 100 percent of the court security officers, magnetometers, and security measures at courthouse entrances.

Appendix I. Objectives, Scope, and Methodology

Objectives, Scope and Methodology

We examined the unique judicial structure of American Samoa and identified issues associated with establishing a federal court in American Samoa. Specifically, the objectives of our review were to discuss:

(1) the current system and structure for adjudicating matters of federal law arising in American Samoa and how it compares to those in the Commonwealth of the Northern Mariana Islands (CNMI), Guam, and the U.S. Virgin Islands (USVI);
(2) the reasons that have been offered for or against changing the current system and structure for adjudicating matters of federal law in American Samoa;
(3) the description of different scenarios for establishing a federal court in American Samoa or expanding the federal jurisdiction of the High Court of American Samoa if a change to the current system were made, if a change to the current system were made, and the identification of issues associated with each scenario; and,
(4) the potential cost elements and funding sources associated with implementing the different scenarios for establishing a federal court in American Samoa.

To address these objectives, we reviewed historical documents, congressional testimonies, law review articles, previous studies, and cost data from and conducted interviews with U.S. government officials from the Administrative Office of the U.S. Courts (AOUSC), including the Federal Judicial Center, Office of Defender Services, and Probation and Pretrial Services; headquarters and field officials from the Department of Interior's (DOI) Office of Insular Affairs and Inspector General; officials from Department of Justice's (DOJ) Civil Rights Division, Criminal Division, Executive Office for U.S. Attorneys (EOUSA), Bureau of Prisons, and headquarters and field officials from the U.S. Marshal Service (USMS) and

Federal Bureau of Investigation (FBI); headquarters and field officials from the General Services Administration (GSA); officials from the U.S. Attorneys offices for CNMI, Guam, Hawaii, and USVI; headquarters and field officials from the Inspector General offices of the Departments of Agriculture, Education, Homeland Security, Transportation, and Health and Human Services; officials and judges from the Ninth Circuit; and officials and judges from the U.S. District Court ofHawaii, the District Court for the Northern Mariana Islands, the District Court of Guam, and the District Court of the Virgin Islands.

Further, we reviewed historical documents, legal decisions, and court statistical data. We also conducted interviews with government officials from the executive, judicial, and legislative branches of government and residents of American Samoa, including the Governor's Office, High Court of American Samoa, *Fono*, Office of Samoan Affairs, Controller's Office, Office of Territorial and International Criminal Intelligence and Drug Enforcement, Attorney General's Office, and Public Defender's Office. Also, we reviewed relevant legal review articles and position papers and conducted interviews with recognized legal experts on territorial governance issues. These experts were identified through our literature review and based on their having published work in the area of territorial judicial systems, and through our interviews with and information collected from federal government and territorial government officials. The experts contacted were not intended to be representative of all expert opinion on American Samoa judicial issues, but were contacted because they could provide insights on territorial governance issues in general.

We conducted this performance audit from April 2007 to June 2008 in accordance with generally accepted government auditing standards. Those standards require that we plan and perform the audit to obtain sufficient, appropriate evidence to provide a reasonable basis for our findings and conclusions based on our audit objectives. We believe that the evidence obtained provides a reasonable basis for our findings and conclusions based on our audit objectives.

Group Discussions and Public Comments

To obtain insight regarding public views related to objectives 2 and 3, during our October 2007 trip to American Samoa we conducted an open forum of college students and the general public and held group discussions with members of the American Samoa Bar Association, American Samoa Chamber of Commerce, and Common Cause of American Samoa.

SEND US AN EMAIL...AMERICANSAMOA@GAO.GOV

The Government Accountability Office (GAO) has begun work on an engagement for the purpose of providing our congressional requesters with (1) an historical context of federal jurisdiction issues regarding American Samoa; and (2) information on the key options for creating a federal court system to cover American Samoa, and the benefits and challenges of each of the options. This engagement is being performed in response to a request by members of the U.S. House of Representatives, Committee on Natural Resources—Nick J. Rahall II, Chairman; Don Young, Ranking Member; and Delegate Eni F.H. Faleomavaega. As part of our work, we are soliciting the views of the residents of American Samoa regarding options for addressing concerns related to the current organization and jurisdiction of the judiciary in American Samoa as it relates to the handling of federal cases.

Our report will enumerate the benefits and challenges of different options for bringing federal jurisdiction to American Samoa but will not include recommendations. Rather, we will leave it up to Congress to determine what actions, if any, should be taken based on our findings. The options we are addressing are:

(1) establishing a new district court in American Samoa, similar to those in Guam and the Northern Mariana Islands, with a new courthouse, a resident judge, U.S. Attorney, U.S. Marshal, and related support staff;
(2) expanding the District of Hawaii to include a separate division in American Samoa, with a new courthouse, a resident judge, an Assistant U.S. Attorney, Deputy U.S. Marshals, and related support staff;
(3) expanding the jurisdiction of the High Court of American Samoa to include federal matters; and
(4) leaving the current judicial structure and system in American Samoa unchanged.

Send us your thoughts on these specific options or the issue in general to AmericanSamoa@gao.gov

About GAO: GAO supports Congress in meeting its constitutional responsibilities and helps improve the performance and ensure the accountability of the federal government for the benefit of the American people. GAO's mission is to provide objective, fair, balanced, and fact--based analyses for the U.S. Congress. GAO's work includes oversight of federal programs; insight into ways to make government more efficient, effective, ethical and equitable; and foresight of long-term trends and challenges. For more information see www.gao.gov.

Source: GAO.

Figure 3. Flyer Distributed in American Samoa

We also established an e-mail account (i.e., americansamoa@gao.gov) and received 62 comments from October 2007 to January 2008 regarding the general public's views on possible scenarios for establishing a federal court in American Samoa or expanding the federal jurisdiction of the High Court of American Samoa. At all discussions and interviews in American Samoa we distributed flyers (see figure 3) which solicited views to the e-mail account regarding the possible scenarios for establishing a federal court in American Samoa or expanding the federal jurisdiction of the High Court of American Samoa.

Emails received were included in our analysis, except those which did not address the issue of a federal court or only posed questions without further elaboration. We did not independently evaluate the merits of the respondents' comments. However, we did group and list the comments by topic. With some exceptions, such as responses that were irrelevant or unclear, substantially all of the comments received were categorized. To ensure inclusiveness and avoid subjectivity in presenting the comments, we did not eliminate any comments, even though the comments perhaps were the same as (or very similar to) comments made by another respondent.

The open forum, group discussions, and e-mails were designed to provide broader insight regarding American Samoan public views regarding the establishment of a federal court. Because these comments are based on a nongeneralizable sample of individuals, they cannot be used to make inferences about the American Samoan population overall. While these views cannot be generalized to the population of American Samoa as a whole, they provided us with a better understanding of the range of issues that were important to the members of the local community.

Potential Cost Elements

To address objective 4 on potential cost estimates establishing a federal court in American Samoa, we obtained estimated cost information for scenarios 1 and 2 from federal agencies that would be involved in establishing a federal court. This included obtaining cost information related to three areas: (1) court construction and rent from GSA, (2) judicial branch agency costs from AOUSC, and (3) executive branch agency costs from EOUSA and USMS. To the extent possible, for scenarios 1 and 2 we obtained agency estimates of the relevant cost elements, including build-to-lease construction costs, agency rental fees, salaries and benefits, operational costs, information technology and equipment costs, and space and facility costs. Since the court scenarios were hypothetical and the exact details of the jurisdiction, staffing, and physical facilities are not known, the estimated costs cannot be aggregated to obtain a precise estimate of the total costs for the scenarios. Further, we did not ask GSA, AOUSC, EOUSA, or USMS to estimate the costs of scenario 3 since this would be a unique structure and the federal agencies would have no existing federal structure upon which to estimate costs. To assess the reliability of the estimated costs for scenarios 1 and 2, we talked with agency officials knowledgeable about how the estimates were developed and reviewed relevant documentation, such as building surveys and agency budget documents. We found the data for scenarios 1 and 2 sufficiently reliable to provide estimates of the possible future costs for these scenarios for establishing a federal court in American Samoa, with limitations as noted below.

Court Construction and Agency Rental Cost Estimates Limitations

Based on preliminary estimates and on hypothetical requirements similar to a proposed new courthouse in CNMI, GSA officials stated that the rough estimate of construction costs would be approximately $56 million and that the resulting agency rental fees based on the amortization of the construction loan might range from $80 to 90 per square foot, given a projected court construction award date of March 1, 2010.[86] GSA and other agencies officials told us that these initial estimated costs may deviate widely from final construction costs for several reasons:

(1) more detailed cost estimates are not available until later stages of construction;
(2) the condition of the undetermined site is unknown;

(3) prices in the construction market may escalate beyond what has been anticipated;
(4) the cost adjustment index used for American Samoa, which accounts for 29 percent of the projected construction costs, is almost 10 years old and relied on limited expert opinion; and
(5) American Samoa lacks local skilled labor and finished materials and the shipping and commodity costs at the time of construction are unknown. These factors would influence final construction costs, and thus agency rental costs.

Judicial Branch Cost Estimate Limitations

(1) Salaries and operational expenses were based on costs from fiscal years 2007 and 2008 data and would need to be reevaluated at the time a courthouse was projected to be built for inflationary and other cost escalation factors.
(2) While CNMI and Guam court costs were used to estimate some court costs, the actual cost variation between American Samoa and the other territorial costs is unknown.
(3) Because reliable estimates of the number of civil and criminal cases were not known, AOUSC officials based their personnel and benefits and operational and information technology cost estimates for probation and pretrial services on a percentage of the actual costs obligated in 2007 from the Probation and Pretrial Services Office in Guam, which is a consolidated operation covering both district courts located in CNMI and Guam. AOUSC officials determined the percentage of resources used to support the District Court for the Northern Mariana Islands as a basis for the estimate of costs for an office in American Samoa.
(4) Rental costs were based on GSA space requirements estimated for the proposed courthouse in CNMI.

Executive Branch Cost Estimate Limitations

U.S. Attorney Cost Estimate Limitations

(1) Because reliable estimates of the number of criminal and civil cases were not known, the U.S. Attorney's cost data for scenario 1 non-personnel costs were based on actual fiscal year 2005 and fiscal year 2006 expenditure and allotment obligations for the U.S. Attorney's

Office for the District of Guam. Personnel costs were based on modular costs provided in the fiscal year 2008 President's budget request to Congress.

(2) For scenario 2, first year modular personnel costs represent partial year costs, whereas second year modular costs represent full-year costs.

(3) Rental costs for the U.S. Attorney's Office were based on GSA space requirements estimated for the U.S. Attorney's Office in the proposed CNMI courthouse.

USMS Cost Estimate Limitations

(1) USMS officials assumed that defendant or prisoner transportation costs for a district court in American Samoa are unknown; however, the officials estimated that it would be about the same as costs in the District Court of the Northern Mariana Islands for fiscal year 2007—approximately 65 prisoners received per year and 104 court productions per year from federal detention facilities in Hawaii to American Samoa. If the workload in American Samoa is less or more, then estimated costs will be affected accordingly.

(2) USMS officials assumed there would be no local detention space to house defendants or prisoners, so air transportation costs to federal detention facilities were included. Commercial airline rates were used since the Justice Prisoner and Alien Transportation System does not extend its flights to American Samoa. USMS officials said that commercial airline regulations and costs could not be specified under all defendant or prisoner transport circumstances.

APPENDIX II. COMMENTS FROM THE ADMINISTRATIVE OFFICE OF THE UNITED STATES COURTS

ADMINISTRATIVE OFFICE OF THE
UNITED STATES COURTS

JAMES C. DUFF
Director

WASHINGTON, D.C. 20544

June 4, 2008

Mr. William O. Jenkins, Jr.
Director, Homeland Security and Justice
United States Government Accountability Office
441 G Street, N.W.
Washington, D.C. 20548

Dear Mr. Jenkins:

Thank you for the opportunity to review the draft report entitled *AMERICAN SAMOA: Issues Associated with Potential Changes to the Current System for Adjudicating Matters of Federal Law* (GAO-08-655). The report is informative and provides useful background information about the U.S. territory of American Samoa and its judicial system.

The report describes three possible scenarios for change. The Judiciary does not have a policy position about whether a change is needed to the current structure, nor does the Judiciary have a policy position on whether to expand further the jurisdiction of the High Court (scenario 3).[1] If Congress were to consider establishing a federal court in American Samoa, the Judiciary would not favor scenario 2, which would create a division of the District of Hawaii in American Samoa. Because of the great distance which separates American Samoa and Hawaii, and the infrequency of flights (only one airline flying two times per week), the U.S. District Court for the District of Hawaii and the Pacific Islands Committee of the Judicial Council of the Ninth Circuit have long held the view that this idea is both impracticable and infeasible. If Congress determines to establish federal judicial jurisdiction in the territory of American Samoa and to commit

[1]The Judicial Conference of the United States has no policy position on this question, but the Pacific Islands Committee of the Judicial Council of the Ninth Circuit has historically supported this scenario as long as adequate resources and facilities would be provided to the High Court.

A TRADITION OF SERVICE TO THE FEDERAL JUDICIARY

sufficient resources to create such jurisdiction, the Judicial Conference of the United States endorses the creation of an Article I district court in American Samoa.[2]

The report indicates that consideration of whether to expand the federal jurisdiction of the High Court or establish a federal court in American Samoa is likely to be focused on policy considerations about equity, justice and cultural preservation, and not principally on cost effectiveness. Nevertheless, the report's assessment of costs should be helpful to Congress, especially because it indicates there would not be significant cost differences between the first two scenarios. The report shows there would be substantial costs associated with the establishment of a federal court in American Samoa. It is helpful that the report makes it clear that if Congress were to establish a federal court or expand the federal jurisdiction of the High Court, Congress must provide adequate resources.

Additional technical comments on the draft report will be provided. We appreciate the cooperative efforts of your team in working with the Judiciary on this complex assignment.

Sincerely,

James C. Duff
Director

[2] *Proceedings of the Judicial Conference of the United States*, September 1996, pp. 57-58. GAO's report refers to this same idea as establishing an Article IV court.

Appendix III. Comments from the Department of the Interior

THE ASSOCIATE DEPUTY SECRETARY OF THE INTERIOR
WASHINGTON

JUN 6 2008

Mr. William O. Jenkins Jr.
Director, Homeland Security and Justice
United States Government Accountability Office
441 G Street, NW
Washington D.C. 20548

Dear Mr. Jenkins:

Thank you for the opportunity to review and comment on the draft Government Accountability Office Report entitled, "*AMERICAN SAMOA: Issues Associated with Potential Changes to the Current System for Adjudicating Matters of Federal Law*." (GAO-08-655). The Report provides a clear comparison of the judicial system of American Samoa with the judicial systems of the U.S. territories of Guam, the Virgin Islands, and the Commonwealth of the Northern Mariana Islands.

Currently, the High Court of American Samoa presides over both local issues and specific Federal issues. Because there is no Federal court in American Samoa, matters of Federal law beyond the High Court's authority must be adjudicated in either the Federal District Court of Hawaii (Honolulu, Hawaii) or the Federal District Court of the District of Columbia (Washington, D.C.). As noted in your report (page 20), the Chief Justice in American Samoa has identified the challenges created by the added workload and the piecemeal nature of the High Court's Federal jurisdiction. Such challenges do not exist in the other U.S. territories, because Guam, the Virgin Islands, and the Commonwealth of the Northern Mariana Islands have both Federal and local court systems. If Federal court jurisdiction in American Samoa were altered as determined by the people of American Samoa and the U.S. Congress, the Department would assist, as authorized, in the implementation of new processes.

Thank you again for the opportunity to comment on the Report. If you have any questions concerning the response, please communicate with Nikolao Pula, Director of the Office of Insular Affairs, at (202) 208-4736.

Sincerely,

James E. Cason

Appendix IV. Comments from the Office of the Governor, American Samoa

OFFICE OF THE GOVERNOR

PAGO PAGO, AMERICAN SAMOA 96799

TOGIOLA T.A. TULAFONO
GOVERNOR

AITOFELE T.F. SUNIA
LIEUTENANT GOVERNOR

June 12, 2008

TELEPHONE: (684) 633-4116
FACSIMILE: (684) 633-2269

Serial: 870

William O. Jenkins Jr.
Director, Homeland Security & Justice
United States Government Accountability Office
Washington, DC 20548

Dear Director Jenkins:

Thank you for affording us the opportunity to comment on the GAO report regarding the possibility of setting up a federal court in American Samoa. While this issue has been lingering on for some time, it is evident from the report that the sentiment of the people of this Territory regarding this issue remains unchanged.

We feel that the results of your fact-finding mission reflect a relatively fair depiction of the general feeling and attitude towards this issue. It is only our intention that we impress upon you again our position that the Samoan land tenure and matai systems are very much vital to the Samoan way of life, and so we must make sure that in our efforts to provide federal justice we do not place it in danger. It is, therefore, incumbent upon the GAO, as the investigative arm of the United States Congress, that the challenges a federal court presents to the Samoan way of life is presented in a clear and distinct manner to the members of Congress, especially our serious concerns on the potential impact it can have on our land tenure and matai system that is the backbone of our Samoan culture and way of life.

Should you require further comments or information from our Office, please feel free to contact us. Thank you for your assistance and work in this matter and we apologize for the delay in responding.

Sincerely,

M. TALAIMALO UIAGALELEI
Assistant Legal Counsel

cc: Toetasi Tuiteleapaga, Chief Legal Counsel
Christopher Conrad
Amy Sheller

Executive Office Building-Third Floor * P.O. Box 485 * Pago Pago, American Samoa 96799

APPENDIX V. HISTORY AND DEVELOPMENT OF THE JUDICIAL SYSTEM IN AMERICAN SAMOA

Overview

American Samoa consists of seven islands located about 2,600 miles southwest of Hawaii and about 1,600 miles from New Zealand. American Samoa Department of Commerce data indicate that in 2005, the population of American Samoa was about 65,500. Ethnically, Samoans constitute the vast majority of the population in American Samoa; about 31 percent of the population was born in the independent nation of Samoa.[87]

The Samoan islands were originally settled about 1000 B.C. by Polynesians.[88]During the nineteenth century, Germany, Great Britain, and the United States developed commercial and military pursuits in Samoa, and in 1899 the three powers divided their authority over the islands, as Germany and Great Britain renounced all rights to Tutuila and the other Samoan islands east of Longitude 171 degrees west of Greenwich, and the United States renounced all rights to the western islands.[89]On February 19, 1900, President McKinley issued an Executive Order placing control of the islands under the authority of the Department of the Navy, and on the same day, the Secretary of the Navy issued an order providing that the islands were established into a Naval Station, to be known as the Naval Station, Tutuila, and to be under the command of a Commandant.[90]On April 17, 1900, the high chiefs of Tutuila formally ceded the islands of Tutuila and Aunuu to the United States, and on July 16, 1904, the high chief of Manua ceded the islands of Tau, Olosega, Ofu, and Rose to the United States.[91]The Deeds of Cession were not formally accepted by the United States until 1929 when Congress, by joint resolution, accepted and ratified them and provided that "until Congress shall provide for the government of such islands, all civil, judicial, and military powers shall be vested in such person or persons and shall be exercised in such manner as the President of the United States shall direct…."[92]

In 1951, President Truman transferred the authority to govern American Samoa from the Secretary of the Navy to the Secretary of the Interior.[93]The Secretary of the Interior subsequently issued an order to delimit the extent and nature of the authority of the American Samoa government, which provided for a Governor and an independent judicial branch.[94]American Samoa ratified a Constitution, which went into effect on October 17, 1960, and a revised Constitution went into effect on July 1, 1967.[95]The Constitution provides for legislative, judicial, and executive branches. The legislature, called the *Fono*, consists of a House of Representatives and Senate. The House of Representatives is composed of twenty members popularly elected from representative districts.[96]The Senate is composed of eighteen members, each of whom must be *matai* and elected in accordance with Samoan custom by the city councils of the counties that the member is to represent.[97]The 1967 Constitution provided that the executive branch was to consist of a Governor, to be appointed by the Secretary of the Interior.[98]In 1977, the Secretary of the Interior superseded this provision by issuing an order providing that the Governor and Lieutenant Governor were to be popularly elected.[99]The Governor's veto power is similar to that of the U.S. President, except that if the Governor vetoes a bill and the legislature overrides the veto with a two-thirds majority of each house, the Governor, if still disapproving of the bill, may submit it to the Secretary of the Interior, who has the ultimate authority to decide if the legislation becomes law.[100]The Constitution also provides for a judicial branch, which consists of the High Court, local district courts, and other courts that may be created by law.[101]In 1983, Congress provided that the Constitution of American Samoa may only be amended by an act of Congress.[102]

American Samoa has limited representation in Congress. In 1970, the American Samoa legislature created the Office of the American Samoa Delegate-at-Large, which was to provide American Samoa with official representation in Washington, D.C.[103]In 1978, Congress recognized the delegate from American Samoa and accorded the delegate status equivalent to that of the delegates from Guam and the U.S. Virgin Islands. As such, the delegate from American Samoa has all congressional privileges, including a vote in committee, except a vote in Congress as a whole.[104]

Although certain characteristics of the court system in American Samoa have been modified over time, the court system continues to resemble the system established by the first Commandant of the Naval Station in 1900. Although the village courts are no longer used, the High Court and the local district court remain in place, with the same basic division of jurisdiction, such that the High Court has jurisdiction over major local matters, including matters involving land and *matai* titles, and the local district court has jurisdiction over minor local matters, such as misdemeanor criminal cases and civil cases in which the amount in controversy does not exceed $5,000. While new avenues to appeal decisions of the High Court have been established, the appellate process within the American Samoa judiciary remains similar, with the appellate division of the High Court maintaining jurisdiction over decisions of the other High Court divisions and the local district court. Further, although the judges were initially appointed by the Governor, since 1931, the Chief Justice of the High Court has been appointed by the President's delegate, first the Secretary of the Navy and then the Secretary of the Interior.

Jurisdiction

In 1900, the first Commandant of the Naval Station, Commander Benjamin Tilley, issued Regulation No. 5, which established a system of courts in American Samoa.[105] The system of courts consisted of village courts, local district courts, and the High Court.[106] The village courts had jurisdiction over minor civil and criminal cases involving Samoans.[107] The local district courts had jurisdiction over more significant cases and cases involving non-Samoans.[108] The High Court had exclusive jurisdiction over major cases involving sums over $250 or criminal penalties over 6 months and all cases involving real property, treason, murder, and offenses committed within the Naval Station.[109] According to a former Naval Governor of American Samoa, the village and local district courts had a case load generally consisting of cases involving offenses such as acts of physical violence, burglary, larceny, sex offenses, desertion, failure to pay taxes, traffic offenses, trespass, nonsupport of wife, and disorderly conduct.[110] At the same time, the High Court mostly handled land and *matai* title disputes.[111]

In 1952, the judiciary of American Samoa underwent a major reorganization. The village courts were no longer used, and their jurisdiction was transferred to the local district courts.[112] The High Court was reorganized into three divisions: appellate, probate, and trial.[113]

The structure of the High Court has continued to change over time, and jurisdiction over certain matters has been transferred between divisions. By 1969, local law had added to the High Court a fourth division, the land and titles division, which was to handle disputes related to land and *matai* titles.[114] In 1979, local law eliminated the probate division and transferred such jurisdiction to the trial division of the High Court.[115] In 2000, local law established a family, drug and alcohol court division.[116] The law authorized the Chief Justice to transfer from the trial division of the High Court or the local district court to the family, drug and alcohol court division juvenile cases, domestic relations cases, certain domestic violence cases, and certain alcohol and substance abuse-related cases.[117]

In addition to restructuring the High Court, local law has also granted the High Court additional jurisdiction, such as over certain admiralty and maritime matters. In 1975, in response to *Vessel Fijian Swift v. Trial Division of the High Court of American Samoa*, in which the High Court held that it did not have in rem admiralty jurisdiction absent an express grant of such jurisdiction,[118] local law granted the High Court jurisdiction, both in personam and in rem, over admiralty and maritime matters in common law.[119]In 1982, the U.S. District Court of Hawaii confirmed that the High Court could exercise both in rem and in personam jurisdiction in admiralty and maritime cases.[120]Although the High Court has jurisdiction over matters of admiralty and maritime common law, the High Court does not necessarily have jurisdiction over actions arising under federal maritime statutes, unless explicitly provided by federal law.[121]Federal law has so provided in, for example, the statute governing maritime commercial instruments and liens.[122]

Throughout the 1960s and 1970s, and again in the early 2000s, federal law also provided that the High Court has jurisdiction over cases arising under certain other federal statutes. For example, the High Court has been granted jurisdiction over cases arising under certain federal statutes governing grain standards,[123] pesticide control,[124] animal welfare,[125] animal and plant health,[126] and poultry and meat inspection.[127]

Thus, current law provides that the High Court and local district court have jurisdiction over all local matters and certain federal matters. The High Court is composed of the trial; land and titles; family, drug and alcohol; and appellate divisions. The trial division has jurisdiction over civil cases in which the amount in controversy exceeds $5,000 (except land and *matai* title matters), criminal cases in which a felony is charged, admiralty and maritime matters, juvenile cases, probate, domestic relations except adoptions and certain child and spousal support cases, all writs, and any matter not otherwise provided for in statute.[128]The land and titles division has jurisdiction over all matters relating to *matai* titles and all controversies relating to land.[129]The family, drug and alcohol court division has jurisdiction over the following types of cases transferred from the trial division or the local district court: juvenile cases, including traffic offenses; domestic relations cases; domestic violence crimes except homicides and other Class A felonies; and criminal cases in which alcohol or other substance abuse is involved, including serious traffic offenses, except cases charging possession of a controlled substance with intent to distribute.[130]The appellate division has appellate jurisdiction over all final decisions of the trial and land and titles divisions, appellate jurisdiction over all local district court and administrative decisions, and appeals of other matters specifically provided for by statute.[131] The local district court retains jurisdiction over civil cases in which the amount in controversy does not exceed $5,000 (except land and *matai* title matters), criminal cases in which the offense charged is a misdemeanor or any offense punishable by not more than 1 year of imprisonment, traffic cases except those involving a felony, initial appearances and preliminary examinations in all criminal cases, adoptions and certain child and spousal support cases, and certain public health offenses.[132]

Appeals

Beginning in 1900, the appellate division of the High Court had appellate jurisdiction over decisions of the trial division of the High Court[133] and over decisions of the local district courts,[134] and when the land and titles and family, drug, and alcohol court divisions were established within the High Court, the appellate division of the High Court assumed appellate jurisdiction over decisions of those divisions.[135] Initially, the local district courts had appellate jurisdiction over decisions of the village courts,[136] but once the village courts became defunct in 1952, the local district court lost its appellate jurisdiction. As such, current law provides that the appellate division of the High Court has appellate jurisdiction over decisions of the trial, land and titles, and family, drug, and alcohol court divisions of the High Court, as well as appellate jurisdiction over decisions of the local district court accompanied by a stenographic record and appeals based on a question of law.[137] All decisions of the local district court in cases without a stenographic record may be appealed to the trial division of the High Court for de novo review.[138]

The Secretary of the Interior may also exercise appellate jurisdiction over decisions of the High Court. In June 1985, the Church of Jesus Christ of Latter-Day Saints requested that the Secretary of the Interior intervene and overturn a decision of the High Court regarding a piece of land in American Samoa.[139] Though he declined to intervene, finding that such an intervention would undermine the U.S. policy of fostering greater self-government and self-sufficiency, the Secretary of the Interior stated that he had the authority to review the decision of the High Court.[140] When the Church of Jesus Christ of Latter-Day Saints subsequently challenged the constitutionality of the Secretary's refusal to overturn the High Court decision, the U.S. Court of Appeals for the District of Columbia Circuit approved of the Secretary of the Interior's assertion of authority, stating that:

> The Congress has delegated its judicial authority with respect to American Samoa to the President, who has in turn delegated it to the Secretary.... The Congress, that is, could have, so far as Article III is concerned, provided that the Secretary himself would exercise the judicial power in American Samoa. No doubt, the due process clause of the Fifth Amendment may qualify this prerogative in some way. The Secretary might not be able to exercise his authority, nor perhaps even to retain it in dormancy, in a case to which he is a party. But that is a far cry from this case. Here, there is no claim that the Secretary was interested in the outcome. So far as due process is concerned, therefore, he could have decided it himself and there can be no cause of action because the court that did so was subservient to him.[141]

A decision of the High Court may not only be appealed to the Secretary of the Interior, it may also be collaterally challenged by filing an action in the U.S. District Court for the District of Columbia against the Secretary of the Interior for failing to administer American Samoa in accordance with the U.S. Constitution and federal law. This approach was first tested in *King v. Morton* in the mid-1970s.[142]In that case, an individual charged in the High Court of American Samoa with willfully failing to pay his income tax moved for, and was denied, a jury trial.[143]He subsequently commenced an action in the U.S. District Court for the District of Columbia against the Secretary of the Interior, requesting that the court declare unconstitutional the Secretary of the Interior's administration of American Samoa in such a way that denied him the right to trial by jury.[144]The district court dismissed the case for lack of jurisdiction, but the U.S. Court of Appeals for the District of Columbia Circuit held that the U.S. District Court for the District of Columbia could have jurisdiction under the federal question or writ of mandamus statutes, stating that the district court is "competent to judge the Secretary's administration of the government of American Samoa by constitutional standards and, if necessary, to order the Secretary to take appropriate measures to correct any constitutional deficiencies."[145]The court again found that district court is competent to hear challenges to the constitutionality of the Secretary of the Interior's administration of American Samoa in *Corporation of Presiding Bishop of Church of Jesus Christ of Latter-Day Saints v. Hodel.*[146]In that case, the U.S. District Court for the District of Columbia found that, though the Church of Jesus Christ of Latter-Day Saints failed to raise a federal question, the court had jurisdiction to hear valid claims under the Constitution or federal law against the Secretary of the Interior regarding his administration of American Samoa.[147]Thus, current law provides that decisions of the appellate division of the High Court may be appealed either directly to the Secretary of the Interior or challenged collaterally in the U.S. District Court for the District of Columbia, whose decisions may be appealed to the U.S. Court of Appeals for the District of Columbia Circuit and then to the U.S. Supreme Court.

Judges

Beginning in 1900, the Commandant of the Naval Station was the President of the High Court and could appoint others to serve as judges.[148] In 1903, the Commandant created the Office of Native Affairs, which was to supervise the judiciary.[149] The Secretary of Native Affairs, a naval officer, became the chief judge of the local district courts, as well as serving as the legal advisor to the Governor, sheriff of the local police force, and prosecutor.[150] Samoans appointed by the Governor sat as judges on the local district courts and magistrates of the village courts, with lifetime tenure, subject to removal only for misconduct.[151]

From 1931 until 1951, the Chief Justice of the High Court was appointed by the Secretary of the Navy. In 1931, the Governor separated the functions of the judge and prosecutor in the Chief Justice and Attorney General. The Chief Justice was to be a civilian appointed by the Secretary of the Navy,[152] and the Attorney General position was filled by a naval officer.[153] At this point, the Governor ceased to be the President of the High Court, and the Chief Justice was appointed by, and directly accountable to, the Secretary of the Navy.[154] The Chief Justice was able to select associate judges from among the district judges to assist with cases in the High Court.[155]

Since 1951, when administration of American Samoa was transferred from the Secretary of the Navy to the Secretary of the Interior, the Chief Justice has been appointed by the Secretary of the Interior,[156] and since 1962, the Associate Justice has also been appointed by the Secretary of the Interior.[157] In the 1970s, the Secretary of the Interior began appointing federal judges to serve as Acting Associate Justices.[158] About once each year, the Secretary coordinates with the Pacific Islands Committee of the Ninth Circuit to appoint judges to travel to American Samoa to hear appellate cases for approximately a week at a time.

Current law provides that the Chief Justice and Associate Justice are appointed by the Secretary of the Interior and hold lifetime tenure for good behavior, but may be removed by the Secretary of the Interior for cause.[159] The Chief Justice and Associate Justice must be trained in law.[160] The associate judges are appointed by the Governor, upon the recommendation of the Chief Justice and confirmation of the Senate, and hold lifetime tenure, except that they may be removed by the Chief Justice for cause.[161] The associate judges are not required to be trained in law,[162] but rather are appointed based on their knowledge of Samoan custom and traditions.[163]

Also according to current law, the appellate division of the High Court is composed of the Chief Justice, Associate Justice, Acting Associate Justices, and associate judges.[164] Sessions are held before three justices and two associate judges,[165] and the presence of two justices and one associate judge is necessary to constitute a quorum and decide a case.[166] In the case of a difference of opinion, the opinion of the two justices prevails, except in appeals from the land and title division, in which the opinion of the majority of five associate judges prevails.[167] The land and title division is composed of the Chief Justice, Associate Justice, and the associate judges.[168] For land matters, sessions are held before one justice and two associate judges, and the presence of one justice and one associate judge is necessary to constitute a quorum and decide a case.[169] In the case of a difference of opinion, the opinion of the justice prevails.[170] For *matai* title matters, sessions are held before one justice and four associate judges, and the presence of one justice and three associate judges is necessary to constitute a quorum and decide a case.[171] In the case of a difference of opinion, the opinion of the majority of the four associate judges prevails, and if there is a tie, the justice casts the deciding vote.[172] The trial division is composed of the Chief Justice, Associate Justice, and the associate judges.[173] Sessions are held before one justice and two associate judges, and the presence of one justice and one associate judge is necessary to constitute a quorum and decide a case.[174] In the case of a difference of opinion, the opinion of the justice prevails.[175] In the family, drug and alcohol court division, sessions are held before the Chief Justice, Associate Justice or Acting Associate Justice, and two associate judges, and the presence of one justice and one associate judge constitutes a quorum for the trial and determination of the case.[176]

The local district court judge is appointed by the Governor, upon the recommendation of the Chief Justice and confirmation by the Senate,[177] and holds lifetime tenure, although he may be removed by the Chief Justice for cause.[178] The district court judge must also be trained in law.[179]

APPENDIX VI. HISTORY AND DEVELOPMENT OF THE JUDICIAL SYSTEM OF THE COMMONWEALTH OF THE NORTHERN MARIANA ISLANDS

Overview

The Commonwealth of the Northern Mariana Islands, a chain of 14 islands stretching north from Guam, has a total land area of about 185 square miles. The three largest islands are Saipan, Tinian, and Rota. Saipan is about 3,300 miles from Hawaii, or about three-quarters of the distance from Hawaii to the Philippines. According to U.S. Census Bureau Data for 2000, the population of the Northern Mariana Islands is about 69,000, composed primarily of Asians, including Filipinos and Chinese, and Pacific Islanders, including Chamorros, Carolinians, and other Micronesians. About 58 percent of individuals residing in the Northern Mariana Islands are foreign born, and about 57 percent are not U.S. citizens. English, Chamorro, and Carolinian are the official languages of the Northern Mariana Islands.[180]

The Chamorro people are believed to have arrived in the Northern Mariana Islands about 1500 B.C.[181] In 1565, Spain claimed the Mariana Islands as a possession, and in the mid-seventeenth century, Spain began to colonize the islands.[182] During the time of Spanish colonization, the Chamorro population of Guam and the Northern Mariana Islands declined significantly—from between 50,000 and 100,000 when the Spanish first arrived in the mid-sixteenth century to around 1,500 by the time of the Spanish census in 1783.[183] In the late-seventeenth century, Spain removed almost all of the population of the Northern Mariana Islands, with the exception of a small population on Rota that evaded the Spanish, to Guam, so that the islands remained nearly uninhabited until the nineteenth century.[184] In the mid-nineteenth century, people from the Caroline Islands began to migrate to the Northern Mariana Islands, and in the late-nineteenth century, the Chamorros were allowed to return from Guam.[185]

During the twentieth century, the Northern Mariana Islands passed under the control of several foreign powers. After the Spanish-American War, Spain sold the Northern Mariana Islands to Germany.[186] In 1914, Japan occupied the Northern Mariana Islands and became formally responsible for the islands in 1920.[187] In 1944, the United States invaded the Northern Mariana Islands and defeated the Japanese.[188] Subsequently, in 1947, the Northern Mariana Islands, along with the Caroline and Marshall Islands, entered into a trusteeship called the Trust Territory of the Pacific Islands, to be administered by the United States.[189]The Northern Mariana Islands, however, after an unsuccessful attempt to be integrated with Guam, sought a separate relationship with the United States.[190]By 1972, the Northern Mariana Islands had entered into separate status negotiations with the United States, and in 1975 the Northern Mariana Islands and the United States concluded a Covenant to Establish a Commonwealth of the Northern Mariana Islands in Political Union with the United States of America,[191] making the Northern Mariana Islands a "self-governing commonwealth … in political union with and under the sovereignty of the United States of America."[192]The Covenant granted citizenship to residents of the Northern Mariana Islands[193] and stated that the Northern Mariana Islands would approve a constitution that would provide for a local legislature, a popularly-elected Governor, and a local court system.[194]The Covenant also provided for a District Court for the Northern Mariana Islands.[195]In 1977, the Northern Mariana Islands adopted the Constitution of the Northern Mariana Islands,[196] and in 1986 the Trusteeship Agreement establishing the Trust Territory of the Pacific Islands was dissolved, making the Covenant fully effective.[197]

The court system in the Northern Mariana Islands has developed in such a way that, over time, the local courts were granted additional responsibility and autonomy. For example, although the district court initially had jurisdiction over certain local matters, such jurisdiction was transferred from the District Court for the Northern Mariana Islands to the local Superior Court. Similarly, appellate jurisdiction over decisions of the Superior Court was transferred from the District Court for the Northern Mariana Islands to the newly-created local Supreme Court. Further, the appellate jurisdiction of the U.S. Court of Appeals for the Ninth Circuit over decisions of the Supreme Court expired, so that the U.S. Supreme Court has the same appellate jurisdiction over decisions of the Supreme Court of the Northern Mariana Islands as it does over decisions of the highest state courts. The current court system of the Northern Mariana Islands is composed of a District Court for the Northern Mariana Islands, which has the jurisdiction of a U.S. district court[198] and a bankruptcy court; a local Superior Court, which handles local matters; and a Supreme Court, which has appellate jurisdiction over decisions of the Superior Court.

Jurisdiction

Beginning in the late 1970s, the District Court for the Northern Mariana Islands had the original jurisdiction of a district court, as well as original jurisdiction over certain local criminal and civil cases and appellate jurisdiction over certain criminal and civil cases. Pursuant to the Covenant, in 1977 Congress established the District Court for the Northern Mariana Islands, granting the court the jurisdiction of a district court of the United States, except that cases arising under the Constitution or federal law had no minimum sum or value of the matter in controversy.[199]The federal law also granted the district court original jurisdiction over all cases that the Constitution or laws of the Northern Mariana Islands did not vest in a local court.[200]Further, the law granted the district court appellate jurisdiction as the Constitution and laws of the Northern Mariana Islands provided.[201]

Pursuant to the federal law, the Northern Mariana Islands immediately acted to vest limited jurisdiction in the local trial court and to define the appellate jurisdiction of the district court. The Constitution of the Northern Mariana Islands, adopted in 1977, established the Commonwealth Trial Court and granted it jurisdiction over all actions involving land in the Commonwealth, other civil actions in which the value of the matter in controversy did not exceed $5,000, and criminal actions in which the defendant, if convicted, could be fined no more than $5,000 or imprisoned for a term of no more than 5 years.[202]The Constitution also provided that, at least 5 years after the Constitution has been in effect, the legislature could vest additional civil and criminal jurisdiction in the Commonwealth Trial Court.[203]In 1978, the legislature of the Northern Mariana Islands also granted the district court appellate jurisdiction over all final judgments, final orders, and final decrees in criminal and civil cases.[204]Thus, at that time, the district court had original jurisdiction over major local criminal and civil cases, as well as the jurisdiction of a federal district court, and appellate jurisdiction over final decisions in criminal and civil cases.

During the 1980s, significant changes were made to the jurisdiction of the courts of the Northern Mariana Islands, as the government of the Northern Mariana Islands vested additional jurisdiction in the local courts, thereby divesting the district court of such jurisdiction. In 1982, the Northern Mariana Islands vested additional jurisdiction in the Commonwealth Trial Court, passing a law such that, effective January 1983, the trial court had original jurisdiction in all civil and criminal cases arising under the laws of the Northern Mariana Islands.[205]Further, in 1988, the Northern Mariana Islands renamed the local trial court and expanded the jurisdiction of the newly-named Superior Court to include all civil actions, in law and in equity, and all criminal actions.[206]The Northern Mariana Islands also established a Supreme Court and provided that, effective in May 1989, the Supreme Court had appellate jurisdiction over judgments and orders of the Superior Court.[207]As a result of these changes, the district court was divested of its original, as well as appellate, jurisdiction over local matters. In 1984, Congress also changed the jurisdiction of the district court by redefining the jurisdiction to be that of a district court of the United States, to include diversity jurisdiction,[208] and the jurisdiction of a bankruptcy court.[209]

Appeals

Appeals from the District Court for the Northern Mariana Islands to the U.S. Court of Appeals

From 1977 until 1984, the U.S. Court of Appeals for the Ninth Circuit had appellate jurisdiction over decisions of the appellate division of theDistrict Court for the Northern Mariana Islands and decisions arising under federal law of the trial division of the District Court, and the appellate division of the District Court had appellate jurisdiction over decisions arising under local law of the trial division of the District Court. The 1977 federal law implementing the Covenant provided that portions of title 28 of the U.S. Code that apply to Guam or the District Court of Guam apply to the Northern Mariana Islands or the District Court for the Northern Mariana Islands, except as otherwise provided in Article IV of the Covenant.[210]Thus, subject to Article IV of the Covenant, which authorizes the Northern Mariana Islands to determine the appellate jurisdiction of the district court, the U.S. Court of Appeals for the Ninth Circuit would have appellate jurisdiction over all final and interlocutory decisions of the District Court for the Northern Mariana Islands.[211]In 1980, the U.S. Court of Appeals for the Ninth Circuit held that it did not have appellate jurisdiction over decisions in cases arising under local law issued by the trial division of the District Court of the Northern Mariana Islands; rather, the Northern Mariana Islands, as authorized by Article IV of the Covenant, had properly vested the appellate division of the District Court with appellate jurisdiction over such decisions.[212]

In 1984, Congress, disapproving of this holding, repealed the statutory provision authorizing the Northern Mariana Islands to determine the appellate jurisdiction of the district court and replaced it with a provision authorizing the

Northern Mariana Islands to determine the appellate jurisdiction of the district court only over the courts established by the Constitution and laws of the Northern Mariana Islands.[213]This amendment made clear that the Northern Mariana Islands could not grant the appellate division of the district court appellate jurisdiction over decisions of the trial division of the district court. Rather, the appellate division of the district court had appellate jurisdiction only over decisions of the local Superior Court, and the U.S. Court of Appeals for the Ninth Circuit had appellate jurisdiction over all final decisions of the District Court.[214]The 1984 federal law also codified the appellate jurisdiction of the U.S. Court of Appeals for the Ninth Circuit over final decisions of the appellate division of the District Court for the Northern Mariana Islands.[215]Once the Supreme Court became operational in 1989, this provision became moot.[216]Thus, from 1984 until the present, the U.S. Court of Appeals for the Ninth Circuit has had jurisdiction over all final and interlocutory decisions of the District Court for the Northern Mariana Islands.[217]

Appeals from the District Court of the Northern Mariana Islands to the U.S. Supreme Court

From 1977 until 1988, the U.S. Supreme Court had appellate jurisdiction over certain decisions of the District Court for the Northern Mariana Islands. The 1977 federal law implementing the Covenant provided that portions of title 28 of the U.S. Code that applied to Guam or the District Court of Guam applied to the Northern Mariana Islands or the District Court for the Northern Mariana Islands, except as otherwise provided in Article IV of the Covenant,[218] such that the U.S. Supreme Court had appellate jurisdiction over any decision of the District Court for the Northern Mariana Islands that held a federal law unconstitutional in a case in which the United States was a party.[219]

In 1988, however, Congress repealed the provision allowing a direct appeal to the U.S. Supreme Court from a decision of a district court.[220]As a result, current law provides that decisions of the District Court for the Northern Mariana Islands may not be appealed directly to the U.S. Supreme Court.

Appeals from the Superior Court of the Northern Mariana Islands

From 1977 until 1989, decisions of the Superior Court could be appealed to the appellate division of the District Court for the Northern Mariana Islands. The 1977 federal law implementing the Covenant authorized the Northern Mariana Islands to determine the appellate jurisdiction of the District Court for the Northern Mariana Islands,[221] and in 1978, the Northern Mariana Islands provided that the district court had appellate jurisdiction over final decisions in criminal and civil cases.[222]As noted above, in 1984, Congress confirmed that final decisions of the appellate division of the district court could be appealed to the U.S. Court of Appeals for the Ninth Circuit,[223] such that decisions of the Superior Court could be appealed first to the appellate division of the district court and then to the U.S. Court of Appeals for the Ninth Circuit. Once the Supreme Court of the Northern Mariana Islands became operational in 1989, it had appellate jurisdiction over decisions of the Superior Court.[224]

Appeals from the Supreme Court of the Northern Mariana Islands

From 1989 until 2004, the U.S. Court of Appeals for the Ninth Circuit had appellate jurisdiction over the Supreme Court of the Northern Mariana Islands. Federal law provides that the relations between the federal and local courts with respect to appeals, certiorari, removal of causes, and writs of habeas corpus are governed by the laws respecting the relations between the federal and state courts, except that for the first 15 years following the creation of the Supreme Court, the Ninth Circuit would have jurisdiction to review by writ of certiorari the decisions of such court in all cases involving the Constitution or federal law.[225]Thus, from 1989 until 2004, the first 15 years of the operation of the Supreme Court of the Northern Mariana Islands, the U.S. Court of Appeals for the Ninth Circuit had appellate jurisdiction over cases arising under federal law decided by the Supreme Court of the Northern Mariana Islands. In 2004, the relationship between the Supreme Court of the Northern Mariana Islands and the federal court system became like that between a state supreme court and the federal court system. Of primary importance, final decisions of the Supreme Court of the Northern Mariana Islands may be reviewed by the U.S. Supreme Court, at its discretion, by writ of certiorari where the validity of a treaty or federal law is drawn into question; a territorial statute is drawn into question on the ground of it being repugnant to the U.S. Constitution, treaties, or federal law; or any title, right, privilege, or immunity is specially set up or claimed under the U.S. Constitution, treaties, federal, or commission held or authority exercised under the United States.[226]

Judges

The length of the terms of appointment for judges sitting on the District Court for the Northern Mariana Islands has increased over time. In 1977, federal law provided that the judge for the district court was to be appointed by the U.S. President with the advice and consent of the Senate for a term of 8 years and paid the same salary as that of a U.S. district judge.[227] The 1984 amendments extended the term of the district judge to 10 years.[228] Thus, current law provides that the district judge for the Northern Mariana Islands holds a term of 10 years and is to receive a salary equal to that of judges of the U.S. district courts.[229]

In addition to the district judge for the Northern Mariana Islands, additional judges may be assigned to sit on the District Court for the Northern Mariana Islands, and the population of judges eligible to be assigned to sit on the court has increased over time. In 1977, federal law provided that, whenever such an assignment is necessary for the proper dispatch of the business of the court, the Chief Judge of the Ninth Circuit may assign justices of the High Court of the Trust Territory of the Pacific Islands or judges of courts of record of the Northern Mariana Islands who are licensed attorneys in good standing, or a circuit or district judge of the Ninth Circuit, including a judge of the District Court of Guam who is appointed by the President; and the Chief Justice of the United States may assign any other U.S. circuit or district judge with the consent of the assigned judge and the chief judge of that circuit, to serve temporarily as a judge for the District Court for the Northern Mariana Islands.[230] In 1984, federal law expanded the population of judges eligible to serve temporarily as a judge for the district court by authorizing the Chief Judge of the Ninth Circuit to assign a recalled senior judge of the District Court of Guam or of the District Court for the Northern Mariana Islands.[231] Thus, current law provides that, whenever such an assignment is necessary for the proper dispatch of the business of the court, the Chief Judge of the Ninth Circuit may assign justices of the High Court of the Trust Territory of the Pacific Islands, judges of courts of record of the Northern Mariana Islands who are licensed attorneys in good standing, a circuit or district judge of the Ninth Circuit, including a judge of the District Court of Guam who is appointed by the President, or a recalled senior judge of the District Court of Guam or of the District Court for the Northern Mariana Islands; and the Chief Justice of the United States may assign any other U.S. circuit or district judge with the consent of the assigned judge and the chief judge of that circuit, to serve temporarily as a judge for the District Court for the Northern Mariana Islands.[232]

APPENDIX VII. HISTORY AND DEVELOPMENT OF THE JUDICIAL SYSTEM OF GUAM

Overview

Guam, at 217 square miles, is the largest island in the Northern Pacific. It is located about 3,700 miles from Hawaii, or about three-quarters of the distance from Hawaii to the Philippines. According to U.S. Census Bureau data for 2000, the population of Guam is about 155,000. Guam's primary ethnic groups are Chamorro and Filipino, and English and Chamorro are the dual official languages.[233]

Guam is believed to have been inhabited by the Chamorro people since about 2000 B.C.[234] In 1521, Ferdinand Magellan landed on Guam; Spain claimed Guam and the Northern Mariana Islands as a possession in 1565, and in the mid-seventeenth century Spain began to colonize the islands.[235] During the time of Spanish colonization, the Chamorro population of Guam and the Northern Mariana Islands declined significantly—from between 50,000 and 100,000 when the Spanish first arrived in the mid-sixteenth century to around 1,500 by the time of the Spanish census in 1783.[236] After the Spanish-American War, in 1898, the United States took control of Guam, and the U.S. Navy became responsible for governing Guam.[237] In 1941, Japan invaded Guam and occupied the island until 1944, when American forces recaptured Guam.[238]

In 1950, Congress passed the Organic Act for Guam, making Guam an unincorporated but organized territory of the United States.[239] The Organic Act granted U.S. citizenship to the residents of Guam[240] and organized a local government, which was to consist of a legislature;[241] a Governor who would be appointed by the President, with the consent of the U.S. Senate;[242] and a district court.[243] Responsibility for the administration of Guam was subsequently transferred from the Secretary of the Navy to the Secretary of the Interior, where it remains today.[244] In 1968, Congress amended the Organic Act to allow for the popular election of the Governor and Lieutenant Governor of Guam,[245] and in 1972 Congress granted Guam a nonvoting delegate to Congress.[246] Although Congress authorized Guam to call a constitutional convention to draft a local constitution in 1976,[247] the proposed constitution was rejected by voters in a referendum.[248]

The court system in Guam has undergone significant changes since 1950. Congress and the Guam legislature have, over time, increased the responsibility and autonomy of the courts in Guam. For example, although the district court initially had jurisdiction over certain local matters, such jurisdiction was subsequently transferred from the District Court of Guam to the local Superior Court. Similarly, while the District Court of Guam had appellate jurisdiction over decisions of the Superior Court for a period of time, such jurisdiction was transferred from the District Court of Guam to the newly-created Supreme Court. Further, in order to provide oversight over the new Supreme Court, Congress originally provided that the U.S. Court of Appeals would have appellate jurisdiction over decisions of the Supreme Court for 15 years after its establishment. However, Congress later repealed this provision, providing that certain decisions of the Supreme Court may be appealed to the U.S. Supreme Court, just as are certain decisions of the highest state courts. The current court system of Guam is composed of a District Court of Guam, which has the jurisdiction of a U.S. district court[249] and a bankruptcy court; a local Superior Court, which handles local matters; and a Supreme Court, which has appellate jurisdiction over decisions of the Superior Court.

Jurisdiction

Beginning in 1950, the District Court of Guam had original jurisdiction over federal cases and some local cases, as well as appellate jurisdiction over certain decisions of the local trial court. In 1950, the Organic Act established the District Court of Guam and granted the court original jurisdiction over all cases arising under federal law, as well as all other cases in Guam not transferred by the Guam legislature to local courts.[250] The Organic Act also granted the district court appellate jurisdiction to be determined by the Guam legislature.[251] The Guam legislature subsequently reorganized the local court system, granting the local Island Court jurisdiction over non-felony cases arising under the laws of Guam, certain felony cases arising under the laws of Guam, all domestic relations and probate cases, and civil cases in which the amount in controversy did not exceed $2,000.[252] Pursuant to the Organic Act, the Guam legislature also created an appellate division of the district court and provided that the district court had appellate jurisdiction over certain civil and criminal decisions of the Island Court.[253]

In 1974, Guam vested additional jurisdiction in the local courts, thereby divesting the district court of such jurisdiction. The legislature passed the Court Reorganization Act, creating a Superior Court, which replaced the preexisting Island, Police, and Commissioners' Courts.[254] The Act provided the

Superior Court with original and exclusive jurisdiction over all cases arising under local law, except for cases also arising under federal law or pertaining to the Guam territorial income tax.[255]The Court Reorganization Act also purported to create a Supreme Court, which was to have jurisdiction over appeals from the Superior Court, and repealed provisions of local law governing the appellate jurisdiction of the district court.[256]The Supreme Court was not established under this law, however, as the transfer of appellate jurisdiction from the district court to the Supreme Court by the Guam legislature was challenged, and the U.S. Court of Appeals for the Ninth Circuit held that the Organic Act of Guam did not provide the Guam legislature with the authority to divest the district court of its appellate jurisdiction.[257]

In response, Congress amended the Organic Act of Guam in 1984 to authorize the Guam legislature to establish an appellate court and to confer upon such a court jurisdiction over all cases in Guam over which a federal district court does not have exclusive jurisdiction.[258]The federal law also provided that, prior to the establishment of an appellate court, the District Court of Guam would continue to exercise appellate jurisdiction over the local courts of Guam.[259]The same law expanded the jurisdiction of the district court to that of a district court of the United States, to include diversity jurisdiction.[260]As an earlier law had conferred bankruptcy jurisdiction on the district court,[261] from 1984 until 1996 the district court had the jurisdiction of the district court of the United States and a bankruptcy court of the United States, as well as appellate jurisdiction over local cases.[262]

The Guam legislature subsequently passed the Frank G. Lujan Memorial Court Reorganization Act of 1992, which created the Supreme Court of Guam.[263]Once the Supreme Court became operational in 1996, the District Court of Guam was divested of appellate jurisdiction over local matters. In 2004, federal law amended the Organic Act to codify into federal law the establishment of the Superior and Supreme Courts of Guam.[264]As a result, the District Court of Guam currently has the jurisdiction of a district court of the United States, including federal question jurisdiction and diversity jurisdiction, and that of a bankruptcy court of the United States.[265]

Appeals

Appeals from the District Court of Guam to the U.S. Court of Appeals

In general, since the establishment of the District Court of Guam, the U.S. Court of Appeals for the Ninth Circuit has had appellate jurisdiction over decisions of the district court. The Organic Act of 1950 provided that the Court of Appeals for the Ninth Circuit was to have appellate jurisdiction over decisions by the district court in all cases arising under federal law, habeas corpus proceedings, and civil cases in which the value in controversy exceeds $5,000.[266]In 1951, Congress repealed this provision and amended federal law governing the appellate jurisdiction of the U.S. Courts of Appeals, providing that the Ninth Circuit Court of Appeals had appellate jurisdiction over all final and interlocutory decisions of the District Court of Guam.[267]In 1982, the U.S. Court of Appeals for the Ninth Circuit held that its appellate jurisdiction extended to decisions of the appellate, as well as the trial, division of the District Court of Guam.[268]In 1984, Congress codified into statute the appellate jurisdiction of the U.S. Court of Appeals for the Ninth Circuit over the decisions of the appellate division of the District Court of Guam.[269]Once the Supreme Court became operational in 1996 and divested the district court of appellate jurisdiction, this provision became moot. Thus, current law provides that final and interlocutory decisions of the District Court of Guam may be appealed to the U.S. Court of Appeals for the Ninth Circuit.[270]

Appeals from the District Court of Guam to the U.S. Supreme Court

From 1950 until 1988, the U.S. Supreme Court had appellate jurisdiction over certain decisions of the District Court of Guam. The Organic Act provided that any party could appeal to the U.S. Supreme Court from a decision of the district court that held a federal law unconstitutional in a case in which the United States was a party.[271]In 1951, although Congress repealed this provision and amended federal law governing the appellate jurisdiction of the U.S. Supreme Court, the right of appeal from the District Court of Guam to the U.S. Supreme Court remained substantively the same.[272]

In 1988, however, Congress repealed the provision allowing a direct appeal to the U.S. Supreme Court of a decision of a district court that holds a federal law unconstitutional in a case in which the United States is a party.[273]As a result, current law provides that the decisions of the District Court of Guam may not be appealed directly to the U.S. Supreme Court.

Appeals from the Superior Court of Guam

From 1950 until 1996, the District Court of Guam had appellate jurisdiction over decisions of the Superior Court. As noted above, the Organic Act granted the district court appellate jurisdiction to be determined by the Guam legislature,[274] and the Guam legislature subsequently created an appellate division of the district court, providing that the district court had appellate jurisdiction over certain civil and criminal decisions of the local court.[275] Pursuant to the 1984 amendments to the Organic Act, the appellate division of the District Court of Guam continued to exercise appellate jurisdiction over decisions of the Superior Court, with the U.S. Court of Appeals for the Ninth Circuit exercising appellate jurisdiction over this appellate division.[276]

Once the Supreme Court, authorized by federal law[277] and established by the Guam legislature,[278] became operational in 1996, it had appellate jurisdiction over decisions of the Superior Court. In 2004, the appellate jurisdiction of the Supreme Court was codified in U.S. Code, to include jurisdiction to hear appeals over any cause in Guam decided by the Superior Court of Guam or other courts established under the laws of Guam.[279] Thus, current law provides that the Supreme Court has appellate jurisdiction over decisions of the Superior Court.

Appeals from the Supreme Court of Guam

From 1996 until 2004, the U.S. Court of Appeals for the Ninth Circuit had appellate jurisdiction over the Supreme Court of Guam. Federal law provided that the relations between the federal and local courts with respect to appeals, certiorari, removal of causes, and writs of habeas corpus are governed by the laws respecting the relations between the federal and state courts, except that for the first 15 years following the creation of the Supreme Court, the Ninth Circuit would have jurisdiction to review by writ of certiorari the decisions of such court.[280] Thus, once the Supreme Court became operational in 1996, the U.S. Court of Appeals for the Ninth Circuit had appellate jurisdiction over the decisions of the Supreme Court. The U.S. Court of Appeals for the Ninth Circuit stated that its appellate jurisdiction over Supreme Court decisions extended not only to decisions arising under federal law but also to decisions arising under local law.[281]

In 2004, 7 years before the expiration of the 15 years after the establishment of the Supreme Court, Congress repealed the provision providing the Ninth Circuit with temporary appellate jurisdiction over decisions of the Supreme Court.[282] Current law provides that local courts of Guam have the same relationship to federal courts as do state courts.[283] Like final decisions of the highest state courts, final decisions of the Supreme Court of Guam may be reviewed by the U.S. Supreme Court, at its discretion, by writ of certiorari where the validity of a treaty or federal law is drawn into question; a territorial statute is drawn into question on the ground of it being repugnant to the U.S. Constitution, treaties, or federal law; or any title, right, privilege, or immunity is specially set up or claimed under the U.S. Constitution, treaties, federal, or commission held or authority exercised under the United States.[284]

Judges

The length of the terms of appointment for judges sitting on the District Court of Guam has increased over time. The Organic Act of 1950 provided that the judge for the district court was to be appointed by the U.S. President with the advice and consent of the Senate for a term of 4 years and paid the same salary as the Governor of Guam.[285]The 1958 amendments extended the term of the district judge to 8 years and provided that the district judge of Guam receive the salary of U.S. district judges.[286]In 1984, federal law again extended the term of the district judge of Guam, to 10 years.[287]

In addition to the judge appointed to sit on the District Court of Guam, other judges may be assigned to sit on the district court, and the population of judges that may be assigned to sit on the court has increased over time. The Organic Act provided that the Chief Justice of the United States was authorized to assign any consenting U.S. circuit or district judge to serve as a judge in the District Court of Guam whenever necessary for the proper dispatch of the business of the court.[288]In 1958, federal law expanded the population of judges that were eligible to be assigned to serve temporarily in the district court by authorizing the Chief Judge of the Ninth Circuit to assign a judge of the Island Court of Guam, a judge of the High Court of the Trust Territory of the Pacific Islands, or a circuit or district judge of the Ninth Circuit to serve temporarily as a judge in the District Court of Guam.[289]In 1984, federal law again expanded the population of judges eligible to serve temporarily in the district court by authorizing the Chief Judge of the Ninth Circuit to assign a recalled senior judge of the District Court of Guam or of the District Court for the Northern Mariana Islands.[290]As a result, current law provides that the Chief Judge of the Ninth Circuit may assign a judge of any local court of record, a judge of the High Court of the Trust Territory of the Pacific Islands, a circuit or district judge of the Ninth Circuit, or a recalled senior judge of the District Court of Guam or of the District Court for the Northern Mariana Islands; and the Chief Justice of the United States may assign any other U.S. circuit or district judge, to serve temporarily as a judge in the District Court of Guam.[291]

Appendix VIII. History and Development of the Judicial System in the United States Virgin Islands

Overview

The U.S. Virgin Islands consists of three main islands—St. Thomas, St. John, and St. Croix—as well as about 50 islets and cays. The islands have a total land mass of about 135 square miles and are located approximately 1,200 miles southeast of Florida and 40 miles east of Puerto Rico. According to 2000 U.S. Census Bureau data, the population of the U.S. Virgin Islands is about 109,000. Based on the same data, of the U.S. Virgin Islands population, about 76 percent is black and 13 percent is white, and though English is spoken at home by the majority of the population, about 17 percent claim Spanish and about 7 percent French or French Creole as their primary language.

The Virgin Islands are believed to have been first inhabited by the Taino branch of the Arawak Indian culture group.[292]The Taino Indians are believed to have been defeated by the Carib Indians, whom Christopher Columbus encountered when he first arrived in St. Croix in 1493.[293]Throughout the seventeenth century, various European powers fought for control of the islands, but by 1735 Denmark governed the islands.[294]With the use of large numbers of slaves, Denmark developed a sugar economy on St. Croix and a trading economy on St. Thomas.[295]

The United States purchased the Virgin Islands from Denmark in 1917.[296]Federal law established a temporary government for the U.S. Virgin Islands, vesting the Governor, who, from 1917 until 1931 was a naval officer, with all military, civil, and judicial powers.[297]The law also provided that local laws in effect at the time of enactment would remain in force and be administered by the existing local judicial tribunals.[298]As such, the legislative branch consisted of two legislatures, one in St. Croix and one in St. Thomas, and the judicial branch consisted of the police courts and district court.[299]

In 1927, federal law provided that all residents of the U.S. Virgin Islands were U.S. citizens.[300]In 1931, the President transferred responsibility for governing the U.S. Virgin Islands from the Secretary of the Navy to the Secretary of the Interior.[301]

Congress subsequently passed the Organic Act of 1936, which established local self-government. The Act provided for two Municipal Councils, one for St. Croix and one for St. Thomas and St. John, which were to meet once a year to enact legislation that would apply to the Virgin Islands as a whole;[302] a Governor, to be appointed by the President with the advice and consent of the Senate, who was to act under the supervision of the Secretary of the Interior;[303] and a District Court of the Virgin Islands and such inferior courts as the local legislature may determine.[304]The Revised Organic Act of 1954 largely maintained the governmental structure from the prior Organic Act, except that it established a unified legislature for the U.S. Virgin Islands.[305]In 1968, federal law provided that the Governor was to be popularly elected,[306] and in 1972, federal law granted the U.S. Virgin Islands a nonvoting delegate to Congress.[307]Although Congress authorized the U.S. Virgin Islands to convene a constitutional convention to draft a constitution, [308] the proposed constitutions were rejected by voters.[309]

The court system in the U.S. Virgin Islands has changed over time, with the local courts gradually gaining increased responsibility and autonomy. For example, though the local trial court previously exercised jurisdiction over certain local issues, in the 1970s and early 1980s the local trial court was granted concurrent jurisdiction with the district court over additional local cases, and by 1994 the local trial court had been granted exclusive jurisdiction over local cases. Similarly, while the District Court of the Virgin Islands had appellate jurisdiction over decisions of the Superior Court for a period of time, in 2007 such jurisdiction was transferred from the District Court of the Virgin Islands to the newly-created Supreme Court. The current court system of the U.S. Virgin Islands is composed of the District Court of the Virgin Islands, which has the jurisdiction of a U.S. district court[310] and a bankruptcy court; a local Superior Court, which handles local matters; and a Supreme Court, which has appellate jurisdiction over decisions of the Superior Court.

Jurisdiction

From 1917 until 1936, the local judicial system in the U.S. Virgin Islands operated largely without federal influence. After the United States acquired the Virgin Islands in 1917, Congress passed a law providing that until Congress otherwise provided, local laws were to remain in force and be administered by the existing local judicial tribunals.[311]By 1921, the local judicial tribunals consisted of a district court and three police courts: the Police Court of Frederiksted, the Police Court of Christiansted, and the Police Court of Charlotte Amalie.[312]The district court had jurisdiction over all civil, criminal, admiralty, equity, insolvency, and probate matters and causes, unless jurisdiction was conferred on some other court, in which event the jurisdiction of the district court was concurrent.[313] The police courts had jurisdiction, though not exclusive, over the recovery of specific personal property when the value did not exceed $200, for the recovery of money or damages when the amount claimed did not exceed $200, and over cases in which the defendant confessed without action to certain offenses.[314] The police courts also had criminal jurisdiction, though not exclusive, over cases involving larceny when the value of the property did not exceed $50; assault or assault and battery, except when charged as committed with intent to commit a felony, in the course of a riot, or with any weapon or upon a public officer when upon duty; any other misdemeanor; and any offense over which jurisdiction was specifically conferred upon the police court. The police courts did not have jurisdiction over actions involving the title to real property and actions for false imprisonment, libel, malicious prosecution, criminal conversation, seduction upon a promise to marry, actions of an equitable nature, or admiralty causes.[315]

Beginning in 1936, the District Court of the Virgin Islands had original jurisdiction in federal cases and some local cases, as well as appellate jurisdiction over the local courts. In 1936, the Organic Act established the District Court of the Virgin Islands, granting it jurisdiction over criminal cases arising under local or federal law, cases in equity, cases in admiralty, cases of divorce and annulment of marriage, cases at law involving sums exceeding $200, cases involving title to real estate, and cases involving federal offenses committed on the high seas on vessels belonging to U.S. citizens or corporations when the offenders were found on or brought to the Virgin Islands.[316] The District Court of the Virgin Islands also had concurrent jurisdiction with the police courts over civil cases in which the sum did not exceed $200 and criminal cases in which the punishment did not exceed a fine of $100 or imprisonment of 6 months, as well as appellate jurisdiction over decisions of the police courts.[317] At the same time, the Organic Act authorized the local legislature to provide for a local Superior Court and to transfer from the District Court of the Virgin Islands to the Superior Court jurisdiction over all cases other than those arising under federal law.[318]

The Revised Organic Act of 1954 provided that the District Court of the Virgin Islands had the jurisdiction of a district court of the United States in all causes arising under federal law, regardless of the sum or value of the matter in controversy.[319] The Revised Organic Act also provided that the district court had general original jurisdiction over all causes in the Virgin Islands, except that the local courts had exclusive jurisdiction over civil actions in which the matter in controversy did not exceed $500, criminal cases in which the maximum punishment did not exceed $100 or imprisonment for 6 months, or both, and all violations of police and executive regulations.[320] The Act further authorized the local legislature to grant the local courts additional jurisdiction, to be exercised concurrently with the district court.[321]

Over time, the Virgin Islands government granted the local courts additional jurisdiction, which was exercised concurrently with the district court. In 1976, Virgin Islands law provided that the newly-named Territorial Court had concurrent jurisdiction over civil cases in which the amount in controversy exceeded $500 but did not exceed $50,000 and over criminal cases in which the punishment exceeded a fine of $100 or imprisonment for 6 months but did not exceed imprisonment for 1 year or a fine as prescribed by law.[322] The same law provided that 2 years after the effective date of the law, the Territorial Court would assume jurisdiction, concurrent with the district court, over criminal cases in which the maximum sentence did not exceed imprisonment for 5 years or a fine as prescribed by law.[323] In 1981, local law expanded the civil jurisdiction of the Territorial Court by increasing the maximum amount in controversy from $50,000 to $200,000.[324]

In 1984, Congress further defined the jurisdiction of the District Court of the Virgin Islands and authorized the local legislature to divest the district court of jurisdiction over local matters. Congress amended the Organic Act, conferring upon the District Court of the Virgin Islands the jurisdiction of a federal court, including diversity jurisdiction;[325] the jurisdiction of a bankruptcy court;[326] exclusive jurisdiction over cases involving income tax laws applicable to the Virgin Islands;[327] and concurrent jurisdiction with the local courts over offenses against local law that are based on the same underlying facts as offenses against federal law.[328] The amendments also granted the District Court of the Virgin Islands jurisdiction over all causes in the Virgin Islands not vested by local law in the local courts of the U.S. Virgin Islands, except that the jurisdiction of the district court was not to extend to civil cases in which the matter in controversy did not exceed the sum of $500 or to criminal cases in which the maximum punishment did not exceed a fine of $100 or imprisonment for 6 months, or both, and to violations of local police and executive regulations.[329] In conjunction with this provision, the amendments authorized the legislature of the Virgin Islands to vest in the local courts jurisdiction over all causes in the Virgin Islands over which any federal court did not have exclusive jurisdiction.[330]

The U.S. Virgin Islands government subsequently took action to expand the jurisdiction of the local courts and divest the district court of jurisdiction over local matters. The local legislature provided that, effective in 1991, the Territorial Court had jurisdiction over all civil cases regardless of the amount in controversy, subject to the original jurisdiction of the District Court of the Virgin Islands.[331] Effective in 1992, Virgin Islands law provided that the Territorial Court had jurisdiction, subject to the concurrent jurisdiction of the district court, over criminal cases in which the punishment did not exceed imprisonment for 15 years or a fine prescribed by law.[332] Effective in 1994, the criminal jurisdiction of the Territorial Court was further expanded, as Virgin Islands law provided that the Territorial Court had jurisdiction over all criminal cases, subject to the concurrent jurisdiction of the district court over local offenses with the same underlying facts as federal offenses.[333] Thus, current law provides that the District Court of the Virgin Islands has the jurisdiction of a district court of the United States, including diversity jurisdiction; the jurisdiction of a bankruptcy court; jurisdiction over all matters relating to income tax laws applicable to the Virgin Islands; and concurrent jurisdiction with the Superior Court over criminal cases arising under local law in which the underlying facts are the same as federal offenses.[334]

Appeals

Appeals from the District Court of the Virgin Islands to the U.S. Court of Appeals

Since 1917, decisions of the District Court of the Virgin Islands could be appealed to the U.S. Court of Appeals for the Third Circuit. In 1917, after the United States acquired the Virgin Islands, Congress passed a law providing that appeals were to be made to the U.S. Court of Appeals for the Third Circuit.[335] The Organic Act of 1936 provided that appeals from the District Court were to be as provided by the law in force on the date of enactment.[336] In 1948, federal law provided that the U.S. Court of Appeals for the Third Circuit had appellate jurisdiction over final and interlocutory decisions of the District Court of the Virgin Islands.[337] The 1984 amendments to the Organic Act confirmed that such appellate jurisdiction extended to decisions of the appellate division of the district court, which had appellate jurisdiction over decisions of the Superior Court.[338] Once the Supreme Court of the Virgin Islands became operational in 2007, this provision became moot. Thus, current law provides that the U.S. Court of Appeals for the Third Circuit has appellate jurisdiction over final and interlocutory decisions of the District Court of the Virgin Islands.[339]

Appeals from the District Court of the Virgin Islands to the U.S. Supreme Court

From 1948 until 1988, the U.S. Supreme Court had appellate jurisdiction over certain decisions of the District Court of the Virgin Islands. In 1948, federal law provided that the U.S. Supreme Court had appellate jurisdiction over any decision of the District Court of the Virgin Islands that held a federal law unconstitutional in a case in which the United States was a party.[340] In 1988, however, Congress repealed this provision.[341] As a result, current law provides that the decisions of the District Court of the Virgin Islands may not be appealed directly to the U.S. Supreme Court.

Appeals from the Superior Court of the Virgin Islands

From 1936 until 2007, decisions of the Superior Court of the Virgin Islands could be appealed to the District Court of the Virgin Islands; since 2007, the Supreme Court of the Virgin Islands has had appellate jurisdiction over decisions of the Superior Court. The Organic Act of 1936 provided that the District Court of the Virgin Islands had appellate jurisdiction over decisions of the local courts.[342] The Revised Organic Act of 1954 again provided that the District Court of the Virgin Islands had appellate jurisdiction over decisions of the local courts to the extent prescribed by local law.[343] By 1965, the Virgin Islands legislature had defined the appellate jurisdiction of the district court over the decisions of the Superior Court, providing that the district court had appellate jurisdiction over Superior Court decisions in all civil cases, all juvenile and domestic relations cases, and all criminal cases in which the defendant was convicted, other than by guilty plea.[344] In 1984, federal law provided for an appellate division of the District Court of the Virgin Islands, which was to consist of the chief judge of the district court and two designated judges, provided that not more than one of them was a judge of a court established by local law.[345] The federal law also authorized the Virgin Islands legislature to establish an appellate court,[346] and in 2004, the Virgin Islands legislature did so, establishing the Supreme Court of the Virgin Islands.[347] Once the Supreme Court became operational in 2007, it assumed appellate jurisdiction over decisions of the Superior Court.[348]

Appeals from the Supreme Court of the Virgin Islands

Since 2007, the U.S. Court of Appeals for the Third Circuit has had appellate jurisdiction over the decisions of the Supreme Court of the Virgin Islands. Federal law provides that the relations between the federal and local courts with respect to appeals, certiorari, removal of causes, and writs of habeas corpus are governed by the laws respecting the relations between the federal and state courts; however, the law provides that for the first 15 years following the creation of the Supreme Court, the Third Circuit is to have jurisdiction to review by writ of certiorari the decisions of such court.[349] As such, since 2007, when the Supreme Court became operational, the U.S. Court of Appeals for the Third Circuit has exercised this jurisdiction. In 2022, upon the expiration of the 15 years, local courts of the Virgin Islands will have the same relationship to the federal judicial system as do state courts. Of significance, final decisions of the Supreme Court of the Virgin Islands will be reviewed by the U.S. Supreme Court, at its discretion, by writ of certiorari where the validity of a treaty or federal law is drawn into question; a territorial statute is drawn into question on the ground of it being repugnant to the U.S. Constitution, treaties, or federal law; or any title, right, privilege, or immunity is specially set up or claimed under the U.S. Constitution, treaties, federal, or commission held or authority exercised under the United States.[350]

Judges

Both the number of judges of the District Court of the Virgin Islands and the terms of appointment of those judges have increased over time. The Organic Act of 1936 provided that the judge of the District Court of the Virgin Islands was to be appointed by the President with the advice and consent of the Senate and hold a term of 4 years unless sooner removed by the President for cause.[351] The Revised Organic Act of 1954 increased the term of the judge to 8 years and provided that the judge should receive the salary equal to that of judges of U.S. district courts.[352] In 1970, the District Court of the Virgin Islands was allocated an additional district judge,[353] and in 1984, federal law increased the term of the two judges of the district court to 10 years.[354]

In addition to the judges appointed to sit on the District Court of the Virgin Islands, other judges may be assigned to sit temporarily on the court, and the population of judges eligible to be assigned to the District Court of the Virgin Islands has increased over time. The Revised Organic Act of 1954 provided that, whenever such an assignment is necessary for the proper dispatch of the business of the district court, the Chief Judge of the Third Circuit may assign a circuit or district judge of the Third Circuit, or the Chief Justice of the United States may assign any other U.S. circuit or district judge with the consent of the judge and of the chief judge of that circuit, to serve temporarily as a judge of the District Court of the Virgin Islands.[355] In 1970, federal law expanded the pool of judges that the Chief Judge of the Third Circuit may assign to serve temporarily as a judge of the District Court of the Virgin Islands to include judges of the Municipal Court of the Virgin Islands.[356]The 1984 federal law further expanded the pool of judges eligible to be assigned by the Chief Judge of the Third Circuit to the district court to include any judge of a court of record of the Virgin Islands established by local law and a recalled senior judge of the District Court of the Virgin Islands.[357]Thus, current law provides that, when such an assignment is necessary for the proper dispatch of the business of the court, the chief judge of the Third Circuit may assign a judge of a court of record of the Virgin Islands established by local law, a circuit or district judge of the Third Circuit, or a recalled senior judge of the District Court of the Virgin Islands; and the Chief Justice of the United States may assign any other United States circuit or district judge with the consent of the assigned judge and the chief judge of that circuit, to serve temporarily as a judge of the District Court of the Virgin Islands.[358]

End Notes

[1]For purposes of this report, we discuss four insular areas—American Samoa, the Commonwealth of the Northern Mariana Islands, Guam, and the U.S. Virgin Islands, which are all jurisdictions under U.S. sovereignty. In this report, we sometimes refer to American Samoa as a U.S. territory, although there has not been enacted an organic act, which would define its relationship to the United States.

[2]H.R. 4711, 109th Cong. (2006).

[3] Legislature of American Samoa, *Report and Record of the Joint Legislative Public Hearing on the Issues of Federal District Court Authorization Transfer of Constitution Review Authority* (Pago Pago, American Samoa: Feb. 23-24, 2006). These hearings were conducted in the Samoan language and translated into English.

[4] The district courts in U.S. insular areas are Article IV courts, as they were established pursuant to Article IV of the U.S. Constitution, which provides that "the Congress shall have power to dispose of and make all needful rules and regulations respecting the territory or other property belonging to the United States…." Because Article I of the U.S. Constitution provides that Congress has power "to constitute tribunals inferior to the Supreme Court," and because many tribunals established by Congress were created pursuant to Article I, district courts in U.S. insular areas are also sometimes called Article I courts.

[5] This estimate includes U.S. citizens, U.S. nationals, and foreigners. Neither the U.S. Census Bureau nor the American Samoa Department of Commerce provides data on the number of all U.S. citizens in American Samoa. In 2000, U.S. Census Bureau data indicated that about 32,470 of the total population of 57,291 were born in American Samoa, and thus U.S. nationals. However, the Census Bureau data do not report the number of U.S. nationals who have become U.S. citizens.

[6] A U.S. national is either a citizen or someone who "owes permanent allegiance to the United States." 8 U.S.C. § 1101(a)(21), (22). Citizenship is derived either from the Fourteenth

Amendment to the Constitution ("All persons born or naturalized in the United States, and subject to the jurisdiction thereof, are citizens of the United States") or from a specific statute that confers citizenship on the inhabitants of an area that, although not a state, is under the sovereignty of the United States. No such legislation conferring citizenship has been enacted for American Samoa.

[7] Samoan *matai* signed the Cession of Tutuila and Aunu'u in 1900 and the Cession of Manu'a Islands in 1904. Later, in 1925, the U.S. acquired Swain's Island. 43 Stat. 1357 (1925).

[8] 45 Stat. 1253 (1929) (codified at 48 U.S.C. § 1661).

[9] 48 U.S.C. § 1661(c); Exec. Order No. 10,264, 16 Fed. Reg. 6419 (1951).

[10] 48 U.S.C. § 1662a.

[11] The Governor may serve two consecutive 4-year terms but is only eligible for a third term after one full term has intervened. AM. SAMOA CODE ANN. § 4.0107.

[12] AM. SAMOA ANN. art. III; AM. SAMOA CODE ANN. tit. 3.

[13] In 2006, the High Court of American Samoa had a total of 607 cases filed, which included 162 criminal cases, 112 civil actions, 15 appellate cases, 11 *matai* (chief) title cases, and 27 land cases. The family, drug, and alcohol division had a total of 21 cases.

[14] In 2006, the district court of American Samoa had a total of 7,689 cases filed.

[15] The Chief Justice and Associate Justice may be removed by the Secretary of the Interior for cause. The district and associate judges may be removed by the Chief Justice for cause.

[16] *See*AM. SAMOA CONST. art. III, § 3; AM. SAMOA CODE ANN. § 3.0220. Three justices and two associate judges are needed for an appellate division session. According to a judicial official, since at least one of the justices has been involved with the lower court trial, that justice cannot sit on the appeals. Therefore, federal judges travel to American Samoa to sit on appellate division sessions, which are held about once a year.

[17] The primary categories of land in American Samoa are freehold land, individually owned native land, and family-owned communal land. Freehold land, or lands included in court grants prior to 1900, may be alienated to a person who has less than one-half native blood. However, individually owned land and communal land, which is theoretically under the control of the *matai* (or chiefs), may be alienated only to persons with more than one-half native blood, and such land may be alienated to a person with any nonnative blood only if the person (1) was born in American Samoa,, (2) is a descendent of a Samoan family, (3)lives with Samoans as a Samoan, (4) has lived in American Samoa for more than 5 years, and (5) has officially declared an intention to remain in American Samoa for life. The alienation of communal land also requires the consent of the Governor. AM. SAMOA CODE ANN. § 37.0204.

[18] There have been three political status study commissions created in American Samoa to study alternative forms of future political status open to American Samoa. The first commission report was completed in 1970 and submitted to the American Samoa Legislature; the second report was published by the Office of the Delegate at Large to Washington D.C. in 1975; and the third report was published in January 2007 and presented to the executive, legislative, and judicial branches of government.

[19] *Final Report, The Future Political Status Study Commission of American Samoa* (Jan. 2, 2007) pps. 43 and 46. An unorganized territory is one for which the federal government has not provided self-government by enacting an organic act or mutual agreement, such as a covenant. An unincorporated territory is one that has not become fully incorporated into the United States.

[20] *American Samoa White Collar Crime Assessment,* a Special Report to the U.S. Department of the Interior, U.S. Department of Justice and American Samoa Government (December 1994, redacted version).

[21] H.R. 4711,109th Cong. (2006).

[22] Article III of the U.S. Constitution provides that "the judicial power of the United States, shall be vested in one supreme court, and in such inferior courts as the Congress may from time to time ordain and establish. The judges, both of the supreme and inferior courts, shall hold

their offices during good behavior, and shall, at stated times receive for their services a compensation which shall not be diminished during their continuance in office."

[23] A U.S. magistrate judge is a judicial officer of the district court and is appointed by majority vote of the district judges of the court to exercise jurisdiction over matters assigned by a statute as well as those delegated by the district judges. A full-time magistrate judge serves a term of 8 years. Duties assigned to magistrate judges by district court judges vary from court to court. Magistrate judges may handle certain pre-trial and post trial matters, as well as jury or nonjury civil trials with the consent of the parties and misdemeanor trials with the consent of the parties. District judges must preside over cases involving felony charges.

[24] Pub. L. No. 95-157, 91 Stat. 1265 (1977); Covenant to Establish a Commonwealth of the Northern Mariana Islands in Political Union with the United States of America, Pub. L. No. 94-241, § 101, 90 Stat. 263 (1976)

[25]Pub. L. No. 630, 64 Stat. 384 (1950).

[26]Pub. L. No. 749, §§ 28, 29, 49 Stat. 1807, 1814 (1936).

[27] Federal law provides that the district court has concurrent jurisdiction with the local courts over local offenses that are "of the same or similar character or part of, or based on, the same act or transaction or two or more acts or transactions connected together or constituting part of a common scheme or plan, if such act or transaction or acts or transactions also constitutes or constitute an offense or offenses against one or more statute over which the District Court of the Virgin Islands has jurisdiction…."48 U.S.C. § 1612(c). As such, if an individual engages in conduct that violates both federal law and local law, that individual may be charged with both the federal and local offense in the District Court of the Virgin Islands. For example, if an individual, while engaged in the trafficking of firearms, kills another person with premeditation, that individual may be charged in the District Court of the Virgin Islands with both the federal offense of firearms trafficking and the local offense of murder.

[28] The original jurisdiction of U.S. District Courts is provided in federal law and includes, for example, federal question jurisdiction, which is jurisdiction over civil cases arising under the U.S. Constitution, an act of Congress, or a treaty, and diversity jurisdiction, which is jurisdiction over civil cases filed based on the "diversity of citizenship" of the litigants, such as between citizens of different states or between U.S. citizens and those of another country, in which the matter in controversy has a sum or value that exceeds $75,000.

[29] In 2004, 7 years before the expiration of the 15 years after the establishment of the Supreme Court of Guam, Congress repealed the provision providing the Ninth Circuit with temporary appellate jurisdiction over decisions of the Supreme Court of Guam. Pub. L. No. 108-378, § 2, 118 Stat. 2206, 2208 (2004).

[30]*See* U.S. CONST. art. III, § 2 ("Trial shall be held in the State where the said Crimes shall have been committed; but when not committed within any State, the Trial shall be at such Place or Places as the Congress may by Law have directed").

[31]United States v. Lee, 159 F. Supp. 2d 1241 (D. Haw. 2001).

[32] 18 U.S.C. § 3238. With respect to a federal criminal offense committed by an American Samoan within one of the federal judicial districts, rather than within American Samoa, venue is proper in the judicial district where the crime was committed pursuant to federal law.

[33]United States v. Lee, 472 F.3d 638 (9th Cir. 2006).

[34] Although venue for most cases arising in American Samoa has been established pursuant to the "first brought" statute, venue may otherwise be proper in a district in which part of the offense was committed. For example, in *United States v. Ofoia*, eight residents of American Samoa were charged in the U.S. District Court for the Middle District of Georgia with defrauding AFLAC, which is headquartered in Georgia. United States v. Ofoia, No. 4:03-cr-011 (M.D. Ga. filed Feb. 28, 2003).

[35] For example, in the District of Hawaii, the Criminal Section of DOJ's Civil Rights Division prosecuted several individuals involved in a sex trafficking operation in American Samoa.

United States v. Kuo, No. 1:06-cr-524 (D. Haw. filed Oct. 4, 2006); United States v. Kuo, No. 1:07-cr-225 (D. Haw. filed May 10, 2007). In the District of Columbia, the Public Integrity Section of the DOJ's Criminal Division initiated proceedings against two government officials in American Samoa, charging, among other things, fraud and bribery. United States v. Sunia, No. 1:07-cr-225 (D.D.C. filed Sept. 6, 2007).

[36]*See* 28 U.S.C. § 1391.

[37]*See, e.g.*, Corp. of the Presiding Bishop of the Church of Jesus Christ of Latter-Day Saints v. Hodel, 637 F. Supp. 1398 (D.D.C. 1986), *aff'd by* 830 F.2d 374 (D.C. Cir. 1987); Majhor v. Kempthorne, 518 F. Supp. 2d 221 (D.D.C. 2007).

[38]A bankruptcy court is an operating unit of the district court.

[39] Maritime law is the body of law governing maritime commerce and navigation, the transportation at sea of persons and property, and marine affairs in general. See app. V for a detailed description of admiralty and maritime jurisdiction of the High Court of American Samoa.

[40]*See* 46 U.S.C. § 30511; 28 U.S.C. § 1404(a). For example, in a 2003 maritime case, a plaintiff filed actions based on the same incident in both the U.S. District Court for the Southern District of California and the High Court of American Samoa. 7 Am. Samoa 3d 139 (2003).

[41] GAO, *American Samoa: Inadequate Management and Oversight Contribute to Financial Problems*, GAO/NSIAD-92-64 (Washington, D.C.: Apr. 7, 1992). U.S. Department of the Interior, Office of Inspector General, *American Samoa: Top Leadership Commitment Needed to Break the Cycle of Fiscal Crisis*, Report No. P-IN-AMS-0117-2003 (Washington, D.C.: September 2005).

[42] In March 1993, Governor Richard Lutali of American Samoa wrote a letter to the Secretary of the Interior, Bruce Babbitt, to request that, pursuant to 48 U.S.C. § 1666, Federal Bureau of Investigation (FBI) agents and a DOJ prosecutor be detailed to the American Samoa Government to investigate and prosecute public integrity and other white-collar crimes.

[43] Department of Justice, *American Samoa White Collar Crime Assessment:A Special Report to the U.S. Department of the Interior, U.S. Department of Justice and American Samoa Government*, (December 1994, redacted version).

[44]Statement of A.P. Lutali, Governor of American Samoa, accompanied by Malaetasi M. Togafau, Attorney General, and R. Wendell Harwell, Territorial Auditor, before the House Resources Subcommittee on Native American and Insular Affairs, *Hearing on the U.S. Department of Justice Assessment on White Collar Crime in American Samoa* (Washington, D.C.: Aug. 3, 1995).

[45]Pacific Islands Committee of the Judicial Council of the Ninth Circuit, *Report of the Pacific Islands Committee on Federal Jurisdiction in American Samoa* (Aug. 23, 1995) and *Supplemental Report of the Pacific Islands Committee, American Samoa Legislation* (Dec. 15, 1995).

[46] The jurisdiction was limited to civil and criminal proceedings that were (1) brought by the United States or an officer or an agency thereof arising under the laws of the United States or seeking to collect a debt pursuant to the Federal Debt Collection Procedures Act of 1990, or (2) designated to transmit requests for international judicial assistance arising from foreign judicial proceedings pursuant to treaties or other international agreements to which the United States is a party and which extend to American Samoa.

[47]*See* United States v. Lee, 159 F. Supp. 2d 1241 (D. Haw. 2001).

[48]United States. v. Kelemete, No. 1:06-cr-116 (D. Haw. filed Mar. 1, 2006).

[49] Recipients that expend $500,000 or more a year in federal awards under more than one federal program are required by the Single Audit Act to undergo a single audit. Single audits are audits of the recipient organization—the government in the case of insular areas—that focus on the recipient's internal controls and its compliance with laws and regulations governing federal awards. 31 U.S.C. § 7501-7507; Office of Management and Budget Circular No. A-133, *Audits of States, Local Governments, and Non-Profit Organizations*.

[50] GAO, *American Samoa: Accountability for Key Federal Grants Needs Improvement*, GAO-05-41 (Washington, D.C.: Dec. 17, 2004).

[51] GAO, *U.S. Insular Areas: Economic, Fiscal, and Financial Accountability Challenges*, GAO-07-119 (Washington, D.C.: Dec. 12, 2006).

[52] A material weakness is a significant deficiency, or a combination of significant deficiencies, that result in more than a remote likelihood that a material misstatement of the financial statements will not be prevented or detected. A significant deficiency is a control deficiency, or combination of control deficiencies, that adversely affects the entity's ability to initiate, authorize, record, process, or report financial data reliably in accordance with generally accepted accounting principles such that there is more than a remote likelihood that a misstatement of the entity's financial statements that is more than inconsequential will not be prevented or detected.

[53] There is also some legal uncertainty about the current ability of federal judges to issue search warrants for property in American Samoa because it is outside of a federal judicial district. A proposed change to the Federal Rules of Criminal Procedure, to be effective in December 2008, would authorize a magistrate judge in a district in which activities related to the crime under investigation may have occurred or in the District of Columbia to issue a search warrant for property in American Samoa.

[54] Legislature of American Samoa, *Report and Record of the Joint Legislative Public Hearing* (Feb. 23-24, 2006).

[55] American Samoa code provides that a person charged with an offense carrying a maximum punishment of over 6 months of imprisonment shall be tried by a jury unless he personally waives this right in writing or in open court. The law also provides that the petit jury shall be comprised of six persons, the jury verdict must be unanimous, and *voir dire* of prospective jurors shall be conducted by the court. AM. SAMOA CODE ANN. § 3.0232.

[56] Legislature of American Samoa, *Report and Record of the Joint Legislative Public Hearing* (Feb. 23-24, 2006).

[57] The ethnic limitations apply to communal lands and individually owned native lands, but not freehold lands.

[58] Letter from the Secretary of Samoan Affairs, American Samoa Government, to GAO, dated October 12, 2007.

[59] 28 U.S.C. §§ 1861-1878.

[60] A federal law enforcement official suggested that rather than establishing a federal court in American Samoa, one option would be to designate the U.S. District Court of Hawaii as the proper venue for federal cases arising in American Samoa and provide the U.S. District Court of Hawaii with additional resources to handle such cases. As such, cases arising in American Samoa would be heard by district judges and juries in Hawaii.

[61] At that same time, the Judicial Conference of the United States' position was that if Congress determined to establish federal judicial jurisdiction in American Samoa, and to commit sufficient resources to create such jurisdiction, the conference would endorse the creation of an Article I district court in American Samoa.

[62] Federal Public Defender officials we met with said that it is unlikely that a court in American Samoa would reach the minimum 200 appointments per year required to appoint a Federal Public Defender in American Samoa. In addition, these officials also indicated that it is unlikely that, under the CJA provision that adjacent districts may aggregate their appointments to establish eligibility, there would be a sufficient CJA caseload to support opening of a staffed branch office of the Federal Public Defender Organization (headquartered in Honolulu, Hawaii) in American Samoa. In the past, the Federal Public Defender in Hawaii has represented defendants from American Samoa when brought to trial in the U.S. District Court of Hawaii.

[63] U.S. district courts, with the approval of the judicial council of the circuit, must have a plan for furnishing representation for any person financially unable to obtain adequate representation. Under this plan, a judge can appoint counsel from a federal defender

organization authorized by the court or a panel of attorneys designated or approved by the court—called a Criminal Justice Act (CJA) panel—to furnish legal representation for those defendants who are financially unable to obtain counsel. 18 U.S.C. § 3006A. Where a federal defender organization is established, the CJA provides that panel attorneys be appointed in a substantial proportion of the cases (defined by guidelines as approximately 25 percent of the appointments annually in a district).

[64] The Pacific Islands Committee is a standing committee of the Judicial Council of the Ninth Circuit with an indefinite liaison responsibility to the Judicial Conference of the U.S. Committee on Federal-State Jurisdiction. The Pacific Islands Committee fulfills the oversight responsibilities of the Ninth Circuit Judicial Council and the Judicial Conference of the United States with respect to the judiciaries of the territories and former trust territories in the Pacific, including American Samoa. The specific responsibilities include assisting in the development and provision for continuing judicial education and court professional training, improvement of the administration of justice in the courts of the northern Pacific, and oversight responsibility for judicial education grants from the U.S. Department of the Interior.

[65] Although case filings may grow over time, if the case filings in a district court for American Samoa were similar to those in Guam and CNMI, they would be fairly small. For example, according to the Administrative Office for the U.S. Courts, *2007 Annual Report of the Director: Judicial Business of the United States Courts*, 38 civil and 169 criminal cases were filed in Guam in fiscal year 2007. For the same period in CNMI, 47 civil and 28 criminal cases were filed. By comparison, the District of Wyoming had the lowest total case filings of any district in the 50 states in fiscal year 2007, with 289 civil and 312 criminal filings.

[66] American Samoa would have to be a separate division within the U.S. District Court of Hawaii as a means to maintain separate jury pools between American Samoa and Hawaii.

[67] 18 U.S.C. § 3231.

[68] 28 U.S.C. §§ 3001, 3002(2).

[69] This rental cost was based on an estimated cost of construction of approximately $56 million, assuming a 20-year amortization of the investment.

[70] The housing plan, developed for the proposed new CNMI courthouse for fiscal year 2009, includes about 68,000 rentable square feet for one courtroom, judge's chambers, and office space for the district court operations, U.S. Probation and Pretrial Services, the U.S. Attorney's Office, and USMS.

[71] OMB Circular A-11, Appendix B requires that federal agencies fund, with up-front payments, the cost of inherently governmental features of the space they lease.

[72] Pro se law clerks assist judges in the management of cases filed by litigants representing themselves.

[73] Because reliable estimates of the number of civil and criminal cases were not known, AOUSC officials based their estimates on the actual costs obligated in 2007 for the District Court of the Northern Mariana Islands. Further, AOUSC officials stated that some district court costs may vary by caseload.

[74] GSA officials estimated that a courthouse in American Samoa would require about 32,000 rentable square feet, based on GSA's build-to-suit lease prospectus developed for a new courthouse in CNMI.

[75] Because the number of civil and criminal cases was unknown, AOUSC officials based their personnel and benefits and operational and information technology cost estimates on a percentage of the actual costs obligated in 2007 from the Probation and Pretrial Services Office in Guam, which is a consolidated operation covering both district courts located in CNMI and Guam. AOSUC officials determined the percentage of resources used to support the District Court for the Northern Mariana Islands as a basis for the estimate of costs for an office in American Samoa.

[76] GSA estimated that probation and pretrial services would need about 5,500 rentable square feet for its operations in American Samoa, based on the CNMI build-to-suit lease prospectus.

[77] *See* 18 U.S.C. § 3006A.

[78] Because reliable estimates of the number of criminal and civil cases for American Samoa were not known, the U.S. Attorney's Office nonpersonnel cost data for scenario 1 were estimated based on fiscal year 2005 and fiscal year 2006 obligation data for the U.S. Attorney's Office for the District of Guam. This is a small U.S. Attorney's Office and is responsible for the federal district courts in CNMI and Guam. EOUSA officials told us that CNMI district court obligations could not be separated out from Guam obligation data.

[79] GSA estimated that the U.S. Attorney's Office would need about 15,800 rentable square feet for its operations in American Samoa, based on the CNMI build-to-suit lease prospectus.

[80] Additionally, USMS indicated that it may be necessary to pay incentive bonuses to attract personnel to American Samoa, as well as permanent change of duty station relocation costs.

[81] Cost data are partially based on prisoner transportation costs in the USMS office in Guam.

[82] If radio towers and supporting radio infrastructure do not already exist in American Samoa, then USMS officials said this may result in additional costs.

[83] Based on GSA's proposed CNMI courthouse floor plan, USMS would be allocated 13,935 rentable square feet. If rent ranged from $80 to $90 per square foot, USMS' rent could range between $1.1 and $1.3 million.

[84] If federal defendants were detained pretrial at the Bureau of Prisons' detention facility in Hawaii, there is no charge to USMS for housing. Given the capacity of this facility, USMS officials told us that it may be able to absorb any American Samoan defendants. If necessary, other detention facilities have been available for use (e.g., the San Bernardino County, California jail, the Agana, Guam detention facility, CNMI Department of Corrections, and Guam Penitentiary). Assuming up to 50 American Samoan defendants in USMS custody per year, for an average of 60 days each, the cost of housing at these facilities may range up to $0.2 million based on fiscal year 2007 costs.

[85] Defendant transportation costs may vary depending upon the number of court productions required.

[86] A 1999 study by Hanscomb and Associates recommended that GSA use a territorial cost adjustment index of 1.53 for American Samoa. The report advised that the index should be applied to GSA's General Construction Cost Review Guide cost estimate for Washington, D.C. Applying the 1.53 index to the space program developed for the proposed CNMI courthouse and assuming a construction award of March 2010, the estimated cost of construction is about $46.3 million. Pending research of land values in American Samoa, GSA officials added a $2.9 million land cost assumed for the proposed CNMI courthouse. Design and construction management fees of $3.5 million and 3.3 million, respectively, were also included.

[87] Samoa, formerly known as Western Samoa, is a country consisting of nine islands located about 80 miles northwest of American Samoa.

[88] Mary McCormick, *American Samoa*, *in* SOUTH PACIFIC ISLANDS LEGAL SYSTEMS 433 (Michael A. Ntumy ed., 1993).

[89] ARNOLD LEIBOWITZ, DEFINING STATUS: A COMPREHENSIVE ANALYSIS OF UNITED STATES TERRITORIAL RELATIONSHIPS 414 (1989).

[90] *Id.* at 414; CAPTAIN T.F. DARDEN, HISTORICAL SKETCH OF THE NAVAL ADMINISTRATION OF THE GOVERNMENT OF AMERICAN SAMOA xi (1952).

[91] DARDEN, *supra* note 4, at xi; LEIBOWITZ, *supra* note 3, at 415. The seventh island, Swains Island, is privately owned and was made part of American Samoa by a joint resolution of the Congress approved on March 4, 1925. DARDEN, *supra* note 4, at xi; LEIBOWITZ, *supra* note 3, at 415.

[92] 45 Stat. 1253 (1929) (codified at 48 U.S.C. § 1661).

[93] Exec. Order No. 10,264, 16 Fed.Reg. 6419 (1951).

[94] Secretary's Order No. 2657 (1951).

[95]LEIBOWITZ, *supra* note 3, at 453.
[96]AM. SAMOA CONST., art. II, §§ 2, 4.
[97]*Id.* art. II, §§ 2, 3, 4.
[98]*Id.* art. IV, § 1 (1967).
[99]Secretary's Order No. 3009 (1977).
[100]AM. SAMOA CONST. art. II, § 9.
[101]*Id.* art. III, § 1.
[102]Pub. L. No. 98-213, § 12, 97 Stat. 1459, 1462 (1983) (codified at 48 U.S.C. § 1662a).
[103]LEIBOWITZ, *supra* note 3, at 454.
[104]Pub. L. No. 95-556, 92 Stat. 2078 (1978).
[105]FREDERICK HARRIS OLSEN, THE NAVY AND THE WHITE MAN'S BURDEN: NAVAL ADMINISTRATION OF SAMOA20 (1976).
[106]*Id.*
[107]*Id.* For example, Regulation No. 5 provided that the village courts had civil jurisdiction over "all civil matters between natives when the amount in dispute does not exceed the sum of ten dollars, but [the village courts] shall have no jurisdiction in any matter concerning real property or rights affecting the same." Regulation No. 5, *cited in* Toomata v. Railey, 1 Am. Samoa 623 (1907).
[108]OLSEN, *supra* note 19, at 20-21.
[109]*Id.* at 21.
[110]DARDEN, *supra* note 4, at 12.
[111]*Id.* In 1930, the *Fono* proposed a judicial commission composed of Samoans, intended to handle disputes related to land and *matai* titles. The Governor created the commission, but after 2 years, the Governor noted that all such cases had been brought to the High Court. CAPTAIN J.A.C. GRAY, AMERIKA SAMOA: A HISTORY OF AMERICAN SAMOA AND ITS UNITED STATES NAVAL ADMINISTRATION 237 (1960); OLSEN, *supra* note 19, at 100.
[112]UNITED STATES ARCHIVES, RECORDS OF THE GOVERNMENT OF AMERICAN SAMOA, 1900-1958.
[113]*See*LEIBOWITZ, *supra* note 3, at 451. In 1960, American Samoa adopted a constitution that provided that any change to the laws of American Samoa respecting the courts, including their jurisdiction, organization, and operation, must be enacted by the legislature and approved by the Governor and the Secretary of the Interior. *See id.* at 421 (*citing* AMSAMOA CODE ANNart. III, § 3 (1960)). In 1967, however, when American Samoa revised its constitution, it deleted the review authority of the Governor and Secretary of the Interior over changes to the court system. AMSAMOA CODE ANN. art. III (1967); *seealso*LEIBOWITZ, *supra* note 3, at 421.
[114]*See, e.g.*, Foster v. Fa'amuli, 4 Am. Samoa 3 (1969).
[115]*See In re:* Beaver Family Trust, 17 Am. Samoa 2d 9 (1990) (discussing Pub. L. 16-28, which deleted references in the American Samoa code to a probate division of the High Court).
[116] AMSAMOA CODE ANN. § 3.0501.
[117]*Id.* § 3.0502.
[118] Vessel Fijian Swift v. Trial Division of the High Court of American Samoa, 4 Am. Samoa 983, 997 (1975).
[119]*Id.* § 3.0208(a)(3); *see also* Meaamaile v. American Samoa, 550 F. Supp. 1277 (D. Haw. 1982). In admiralty and maritime law, in rem jurisdiction is the court's jurisdiction over a vessel, such that the vessel itself is made the defendant in order to enforce a lien, and in personam jurisdiction is the court's jurisdiction over a person, such that a legal action may be brought against the owner or master of a ship. *See Meaamaile*, 550 F. Supp. 1277.
[120]*Meaamaile*, 550 F. Supp. 1277.
[121]*See, e.g.*, *In re:* Voyager, 23 Am. Samoa 2d 47 (1992) (holding that the High Court has no jurisdiction to grant relief under the federal limitations-of-liability statute).
[122] 46 U.S.C. § 31301 (defining the High Court of American Samoa as a "district court" for the purposes of the statute); *see also* United Airlines Employees' Credit Union v. The M/V

Sans End, 15 Am. Samoa 2d 95 (1990) (holding that the High Court has jurisdiction to enforce a preferred mortgage lien under federal law).

[123]7 U.S.C. § 87f(h).

[124]7 U.S.C. § 136(*i*).

[125]7 U.S.C. § 2146(c); 15 U.S.C. § 1825(d)(6).

[126]7 U.S.C. § 7736(a); 7 U.S.C. § 8314(c).

[127]21 U.S.C. § 674.

[128] AMSAMOA CODE ANN. § 3.0208(a).

[129]*Id.* § 3.0208(b).

[130]*Id.* § 3.0502(a).

[131]*Id.* § 3.0208(c).

[132]*Id.* § 3.0302.

[133]*See, e.g.*, American Samoa v. Willis, 1 Am. Samoa 635 (1911).

[134]*See, e.g.*, Toomata v. Railey, 1 Am. Samoa 623 (1907).

[135]*See, e.g.*, *In re:* Matai Title Alalamua, 4 Am. Samoa 974 (1974).

[136]*See, e.g.*, Toomata v. Railey, 1 Am. Samoa 623 (1907)

[137]AMSAMOA CODE ANN. §§ 3.0208(c), 3.0309.

[138]*Id.* § 3.0309.

[139]*See* Corp. of Presiding Bishop of Church of Jesus Christ of Latter-Day Saints v. Hodel, 830 F.2d 374, 378 (D.C. Cir. 1987).

[140]*Seeid.*; *see also*LEIBOWITZ, *supra* note 3, at 419.

[141] Corp. of Presiding Bishop of Church of Jesus Christ of Latter-Day Saints v. Hodel, 830 F.2d at 384.

[142]King v. Morton, 520 F.2d 1140 (D.C. Cir. 1975).

[143]*Id.* at 1142.

[144]*Id.* at 1143.

[145]*Id.* at 1144.

[146] Corp. of Presiding Bishop of Church of Jesus Christ of Latter-Day Saints v. Hodel, 637 F. Supp. 1398 (D.D.C. 1986), *aff'd* 830 F.2d 374 (D.C. Cir. 1987).

[147]*Id.*

[148]OLSEN, *supra* note 19, at 21. The title of Commandant was changed to Governor in 1905. DARDEN, *supra* note 4, at 7.

[149]UNITED STATES ARCHIVES, *supra* note 26.

[150]DARDEN, *supra* note 4, at 11.

[151]OLSEN, *supra* note 19, at 20-21.

[152]DARDEN, *supra* note 4, at 11; UNITED STATES ARCHIVES, *supra* note 26. The Chief Justice was a civilian appointed by the Secretary of the Navy from 1931 until 1951, when administration of American Samoa transferred to the Secretary of Interior, except from 1942 until 1946, when, during the period of military government, the Chief Justice was a naval officer. DARDEN, *supra* note 4, at 11.

[153]GRAY, *supra* note 25, at 232; DARDEN, *supra* note 4, at 8, 11; UNITED STATES ARCHIVES, *supra* note 26; OLSEN, *supra* note 19, at 100.

[154]OLSEN, *supra* note 19, at 100; DARDEN, *supra* note 4, at 11; GRAY, *supra* note 25, at 232. The Attorney General was a naval officer with legal training that served as government counsel, secretary of Samoan affairs, government secretary, collector of taxes and revenues, passport officer, sheriff, prison supervisor, manager of the copra fund, and later, chairman of the Board of Samoan Industries, and legislative counsel and administrative officer of the *Fono* of American Samoa. GRAY, *supra* note 25, at 232.

[155]LEIBOWITZ, supra note 3, at 451.

[156]*See id.* at 452.

[157]Am. Samoa Pub. L. No. 7-36 (1962) (codified at AM. SAMOA CODE ANN. § 3.1001).

[158]AMSAMOA CODE ANN. § 3.0220.

[159]*Id.* § 3.1010(a).

[160]*Id.* § 3.1001(a).
[161]*Id.* § 3.1004(d). The associate judges are also subject to mandatory retirement at age 65, unless waived by the Governor. *Id.*
[162]*See id.* § 3.1004.
[163]*See* Charles Timothy Morgan, *Some Observations on the Judiciary in American Samoa*, 18 UCLA L. REV. 581 (1970-71).
[164]AM. SAMOA CODE ANN. § 3.0220.
[165]*Id.*
[166]*Id.*
[167]AM. SAMOA CODE ANN. § 3.0221.
[168]*Id.* § 3.0240.
[169]*Id.*
[170]*Id.* § 3.0241.
[171]*Id.* § 3.0240.
[172]*Id.* § 3.0241.
[173]*Id.* § 3.0230(a).
[174]*Id.* § 3.0230(b).
[175]*Id.* § 3.0231.
[176]*Id.* § 3.0502(c).
[177]*Id.* § 3.1010(a).
[178]*Id.* § 3.1010(c).
[179]*Id.* § 3.1010(a).
[180]N. MAR. I. CONST.. art. XXII, § 3.
[181]ARNOLD LEIBOWITZ, DEFINING STATUS: A COMPREHENSIVE ANALYSIS OF UNITED STATES TERRITORIAL RELATIONSHIPS 426 (1989); Bruce Ottle, *The Commonwealth of the Northern Mariana Islands*, *in*SOUTH PACIFIC ISLANDS LEGAL SYSTEMS 540 (Michael A. Ntumy ed.,1993).
[182]STANLEY LAUGHLIN, THE LAW OF UNITED STATES TERRITORIES AND AFFILIATED JURISDICTIONS 426 (1995); Ottle, *supra* note 2, at 540.
[183]LAUGHLIN, *supra* note 3, at 427; LEIBOWITZ, *supra* note 2, at 522;.
[184]LAUGHLIN, *supra* note 3, at 427; LEIBOWITZ, *supra* note 2, at 522; Ottle, *supra* note 2, at 541.
[185]LAUGHLIN, *supra* note 3, at 427.
[186]Ottle, *supra* note 2, at 428.
[187]LAUGHLIN, *supra* note 3, at 428; LEIBOWITZ, *supra* note 2, at 525.
[188]LAUGHLIN, *supra* note 3, at 428; LEIBOWITZ, *supra* note 2, at 526.
[189]LAUGHLIN, *supra* note 3, at 428-29; LEIBOWITZ, *supra* note 2, at 526-27; Ottle, *supra* note 2, at 541.
[190]LAUGHLIN, *supra* note 3, at 429; LEIBOWITZ, *supra* note 2, at 527-30.
[191]LAUGHLIN, *supra* note 3, at 430; LEIBOWITZ, *supra* note 2, at 529-530.
[192] Covenant to Establish a Commonwealth of the Northern Mariana Islands in Political Union with the United States of America, Pub. L. No. 94-241, 90 Stat. 263 (1976).
[193]*Id.* art. III, 90 Stat. at 265-66.
[194]*Id.* art. II, 90 Stat. at 264-65.
[195]*Id.* art. IV, 90 Stat. at 266-67.
[196]N. MAR. I. CONST. (1977), *reprinted in* Howard P. Willens & Deanne C. Siemer, *The Constitution of the Northern Mariana Islands: Constitutional Principles and Innovation in a Pacific Setting*, 65 Geo.L.J. 1373 (1977) [hereinafter N. MAR. I. CONST.].
[197]LEIBOWITZ, *supra* note 2, at 536; Ottle, *supra* note 2, at 541.
[198] The original jurisdiction of U.S. district courts is provided in federal law and includes, for example, federal question jurisdiction, which is jurisdiction over civil cases arising under the U.S. Constitution, an act of Congress, or a treaty, and diversity jurisdiction, which is jurisdiction over civil cases filed based on the "diversity of citizenship" of the litigants, such as between citizens of different states or between U.S. citizens and those of another country,

in which the matter in controversy has a sum or value that exceeds $75,000. 28 U.S.C. §§ 1331, 1332.

[199] Pub. L. No. 95-157, § 2(a), 91 Stat. 1265, 1266 (1977) (codified as amended at 48 U.S.C. § 1821).

[200] *Id.* § 2(b), 91 Stat. at 1266.

[201] *Id.* § 3, 91 Stat. at 1266. The law provided that the appellate division of the district court was to consist of the district court judge and two other judges to be designated by the district court judge from among the judges assigned to the court, provided that not more than one of them was a judge of a court of record of the Northern Mariana Islands. *Id.*

[202] N. MAR. I. CONST. art. IV, § 2.

[203] N. MAR. I. CONST. art. IV, § 2.

[204] 1978 N. Mar. I. Pub. L. 1-5.

[205] 1982 N. Mar. I. Pub. L. 3-14, § 2.

[206] 1988 N. Mar. I. Pub. L. 6-25, §§ 3201, 3202.

[207] *Id.* §§ 3101, 3102.

[208] Diversity jurisdiction is described in 28 U.S.C. § 1332 and includes jurisdiction over civil actions in which the matter in controversy exceeds the sum or value of $75,000 and that are between citizens of different states, citizens of a state and citizens of a foreign state, citizens of different states and in which citizens of a foreign state are additional parties, or a foreign state as plaintiff and citizens of a state or different states. 28 U.S.C. § 1332.

[209] Pub. L. No. 98-454, § 902, 98 Stat. 1732, 1744 (1984) (codified at 48 U.S.C. § 1822).

[210] Pub. L. No. 95-157, § 4(b), 91 Stat. 1265, 1267 (1977).

[211] *See* 28 U.S.C. §§ 1291, 1292, 1294.

[212] Sablan v. Santos, 634 F.2d 1153 (9th Cir. 1980). The court found that the provision stating that the portions of title 28 that applied to Guam also applied to the Northern Mariana Islands is made subject to Article IV of the Covenant, which authorizes the Northern Mariana Islands to determine the appellate jurisdiction of the District Court. *Id.* at 1155. As a result, the court held that, although the U.S. Court of Appeals had appellate jurisdiction over decisions of the District Court of Guam, the Northern Mariana Islands had the authority to determine that the same provision did not apply to the Northern Mariana Islands and that, rather, the appellate division of the District Court for the Northern Mariana Islands had appellate jurisdiction over the trial division of the District Court for the Northern Mariana Islands. *Id.*

[213] Pub. L. No. 98-454, § 903, 98 Stat. at 1744.

[214] *Id.*; *see also* Gioda v. Saipan Stevedoring Co., 855 F.2d 625 (9th Cir. 1988).

[215] Pub. L. No. 98-454, § 903, 98 Stat. at 1745.

[216] Even after the Supreme Court was established, the appellate division of the District Court retained jurisdiction over appeals that were pending at the time of the establishment of the Supreme Court. *See* Wabol v. Villacrusis, 958 F.2d 1450 (9th Cir. 1992).

[217] 28 U.S.C. §§ 1291, 1292, 1294.

[218] Pub. L. No. 95-157, § 4(b), 91 Stat. 1265, 1267 (1977).

[219] *See* 28 U.S.C. § 1252, *repealed by* Pub. L. No. 100-352, § 1, 102 Stat. 662 (1988).

[220] Pub. L. No. 100-352, § 3, 102 Stat. 662 (1988).

[221] Pub. L. No. 95-157, § 3, 91 Stat. at 1266.

[222] 1978 N. Mar. I. Pub. L. 1-5.

[223] Pub. L. No. 98-454, § 903, 98 Stat. 1732, 1745 (1984).

[224] 1988 N. Mar. I. Pub. L. 6-25, §§ 3101, 3102. Pending appeals continued to be heard by the appellate division of the District Court for the Northern Mariana Islands. *See Wabol*, 958 F.2d 1450.

[225] Pub. L. No. 95-157, § 4, 91 Stat. at 1266 (codified at 48 U.S.C. § 1824).

[226] 28 U.S.C. § 1257.

[227] Pub. L. No. 95-157, § 1(b)(1), 91 Stat. at 1265.

[228] Pub. L. No. 98-454, § 901(a), 98 Stat. 1732, 1744 (1984).

[229]48 U.S.C. § 1821(b)(1).
[230]Pub. L. No. 95-157, § 1(b)(2), 91 Stat. at 1265.
[231]Pub. L. No. 98-454, § 901(b), 98 Stat. 1732, 1744 (1984).
[232]48 U.S.C. § 1821(b)(2).
[233]GUAM CODE. ANN. tit. 1, §706.
[234]ARNOLD LEIBOWITZ, DEFINING STATUS: A COMPREHENSIVE ANALYSIS OF UNITED STATES TERRITORIAL RELATIONSHIPS315 (1989); Mary McCormick, *Guam*, *in* SOUTH PACIFIC ISLANDS LEGAL SYSTEMS518, 518 (1993).
[235]STANLEY LAUGHLIN, THE LAWS OF UNITED STATES TERRITORIES ANDAFFILIATED JURISDICTIONS399 (1995); LEIBOWITZ, *supra* note 2, at 316; McCormick, *supra* note 2, at 518.
[236]LAUGHLIN, *supra* note 3, at 400; LEIBOWITZ, *supra* note 2, at 316.
[237]LAUGHLIN,*supra* note 3, at 400; LEIBOWITZ, *supra* note 2, at 318-19; McCormick, *supra* note 2, at 518.
[238]LAUGHLIN, *supra note 3, at*401-02; LEIBOWITZ, *supra* note 2, at323.
[239]Pub. L. No. 630, § 3, 64 Stat. 384, 384 (1950).
[240]*Id.* § 4, 64 Stat. at 384.
[241]*Id.* § 10, 64 Stat. at 387.
[242]*Id.* § 7, 64 Stat. at 387.
[243]*Id.* § 22, 64 Stat. at 389-90.
[244]CAPTAIN J.A.C. GRAY, AMERIKA SAMOA: A HISTORY OF AMERICAN SAMOA AND ITS UNITED STATES NAVAL ADMINISTRATION258 (1960); McCormick, *supra* note 2, at 519.
[245]Pub. L. No. 90-497, § 6, 82 Stat. 842, 842-43 (codified at 48 U.S.C. § 1422).
[246]Pub. L. No. 92-271, § 1, 86 Stat. 118, 118 (codified at 48 U.S.C. § 1711).
[247]Pub. L. No. 94-584, § 2, 90 Stat. 2899, 2899 (1976).
[248]McCormick, *supra* note 2, at 519.
[249] The original jurisdiction of U.S. district courts is provided in federal law and includes, for example, federal question jurisdiction, which is jurisdiction over civil cases arising under the U.S. Constitution, an act of Congress, or a treaty, and diversity jurisdiction, which is jurisdiction over civil cases filed based on the "diversity of citizenship" of the litigants, such as between citizens of different states or between U.S. citizens and those of another country, in which the matter in controversy has a sum or value that exceeds $75,000. 28 U.S.C. §§ 1331, 1332.
[250]Pub. L. No. 630, § 22(a), 64 Stat. 384, 389-90 (1950).
[251]*Id.*
[252] Guam Pub. L. No. 17, § 1 (1951), *cited in* Corn v. Guam Coral Co., 318 F.2d 622, 624 (9th Cir. 1963).
[253]*Id.* In 1958, Congress approved this measure by amending section 22(a) of the Organic Act to require that appeals to the District Court be heard by an appellate division consisting of three judges. The judges were to consist of the district court judge and two other judges to be designated by the district court judge from among the judges assigned to the court, provided that not more than one of them is a judge of a court of record of Guam. Pub. L. No. 85-444, § 2, 72 Stat. 178, 179 (1958).
[254] Guam Pub. L. No. 12-85 (1974), *cited in* Territory of Guam v. Olsen, 431 U.S. 195, 197 (1977).
[255]*Id.* The law does not explicitly state that the jurisdiction of the Superior Court over cases arising under local law is exclusive of the district court. *See id.* However, because the district court only has jurisdiction over cases arising under local law if such jurisdiction is not transferred to courts created by the Guam legislature, and the Guam legislature created local courts with jurisdiction over cases arising under local law, the District Court does not have jurisdiction over such cases. *See* Agana Bay Development Co. v. Supreme Court of Guam, 529 F.2d 952, 953 (9th Cir. 1976), *rev'd sub nom. on other grounds*, Guam v. Olsen, 540 F.2d 1011 (9th Cir. 1976) (en banc), *aff'd*, 431 U.S. 195 (1977).

[256]Guam Pub. L. No. 12-85 (1974), *cited in* Territory of Guam v. Olsen, 431 U.S.at 197-98.
[257]Guam v. Olsen, 540 F.2d at 1012 (en banc), *aff'd*, 431 U.S. 195 (1977).
[258]Pub. L. No. 98-454, § 801, 98 Stat. 1732, 1742 (1984).
[259]*Id.*
[260] Diversity jurisdiction is described in 28 U.S.C. § 1332 and includes jurisdiction over civil actions in which the matter in controversy exceeds the sum or value of $75,000 and that are between citizens of different states, citizens of a state and citizens of a foreign state, citizens of different states and in which citizens of a foreign state are additional parties, or a foreign state as plaintiff and citizens of a state or different states. 28 U.S.C. § 1332.
[261]Pub. L. No. 95-598, § 335, 92 Stat. 2549, 2680 (1978).
[262]Pub. L. No. 98-454, § 801, 98 Stat. at 1741.
[263]Guam Pub. L. No. 21-147 (codified in part at GUAM CODE ANN. tit. 7, § 3101).
[264]Pub. L. No. 108-378, § 1, 118 Stat. 2206, 2206-07 (2004).
[265]48 U.S.C. § 1424(b).
[266]Pub. L. No. 630, § 23(a), 64 Stat. 384, 390 (1950).
[267] Pub. L. No. 248, §§ 48, 49, 50, 65 Stat. 710, 726-27 (1951) (codified at 28 U.S.C. §§ 1291, 1292, 1294).
[268]Corn v. Guam Coral Co., 318 F.2d 622 (9th Cir. 1963).
[269]Pub. L. No. 98-454, § 801, 98 Stat. 1732, 1743 (1984) (codified at 48 U.S.C. § 1424-3(c)).
[270]28 U.S.C. §§1291, 1292, 1294.
[271]Pub. L. No. 630, § 23(b), 64 Stat. at 390.
[272] Pub. L. No. 248, § 47, 65 Stat. 710, 726 (1951), *repealed by* Pub. L. No. 100-352, § 1, 102 Stat. 662 (1988).
[273]Pub. L. No. 100-352, § 3, 102 Stat. 662 (1988).
[274]Pub. L. No. 630, § 22(a), 64 Stat. at 389-90.
[275] Guam Pub. L. No. 17, § 1 (1951), *cited in* Corn v. Guam Coral Co., 318 F.2d 622, 624 (9th Cir. 1963).
[276]Pub. L. No. 98-454, § 801, 98 Stat. 1732, 1742 (1984).
[277]*Seeid.* (codified as amended at 48 U.S.C. § 1424-3(a)).
[278]Guam Pub. L. No. 21-147 (codified in part at GUAM CODE ANN. tit. 7, § 3101).
[279]Pub. L. No. 108-378, § 1, 118 Stat. 2206 (2004) (codified at 48 U.S.C. § 1424-1(a)(2)).
[280] Pub. L. No. 98-454, § 801, 98 Stat. 1732, 1742 (1984) (codified as amended at 48 U.S.C. § 1424-2).
[281]*See, e.g.*, EIE Guam Corp. v. Supreme Court of Guam, 191 F.3d 1123 (9th Cir. 1999).
[282]Pub. L. No. 108-378, § 2, 118 Stat. 2206, 2208 (2004).
[283]48 U.S.C. § 1424-2.
[284]28 U.S.C. § 1257.
[285]Pub. L. No. 630, § 24(a), 64 Stat. 384, 390 (1950).
[286]Pub. L. No. 85-444, § 3, 72 Stat. 178, 179 (1958).
[287]Pub. L. No. 98-454, § 802, 98 Stat. 1732, 1743 (1984) (codified at 48 U.S.C. § 1424b(a)).
[288]Pub. L. No. 630, § 24(a), 64 Stat. 384, 390 (1950).
[289]Pub. L. No. 85-444, § 3, 72 Stat. 178, 179 (1958).
[290]Pub. L. No. 98-454, § 802, 98 Stat. 1732, 1743 (1984).
[291]48 U.S.C. § 1424b(a).
[292]ARNOLD LEIBOWITZ, DEFINING STATUS: A COMPREHENSIVE ANALYSIS OF UNITED STATES TERRITORIAL RELATIONSHIPS 237-38 (1989).
[293]*Id.*
[294]*Id.* at 242-43.
[295]*Id.*
[296]*Id.* at 233.
[297]Pub. L. No. 380, § 1, 39 Stat. 1132 (1917); LEIBOWITZ, *supra* note 1, at 253.
[298]Pub. L. No. 380, § 2, 39 Stat. at 1132.
[299]LEIBOWITZ, *supra* note 1, at 253.

[300]Pub. L. No. 640, 44 Stat. 1234 (1927).
[301]Exec. Order No. 5566 (Feb. 27, 1931), *cited in*LEIBOWITZ, *supra* note 1, at 255.
[302]Pub. L. No. 749, §§ 5, 6, 7, 49 Stat. 1807, 1807-08 (1936).
[303]*Id.* § 20, 49 Stat. at 1812.
[304]*Id.* § 25, 49 Stat. at 1813.
[305]Pub. L. No. 517, § 5, 68 Stat. 497, 498 (1954).
[306]Pub. L. No. 90-496, § 4, 82 Stat. 837, 837 (1968).
[307]Pub. L. No. 92-271, § 1, 86 Stat. 118, 118 (1972).
[308]Pub. L. No. 94-584, 90 Stat. 2899 (1976).
[309]STANLEY LAUGHLIN, THE LAWS OF UNITED STATES TERRITORIES AND AFFILIATED JURISDICTIONS 380 (1995).
[310] The original jurisdiction of U.S. district courts is provided in federal law and includes, for example, federal question jurisdiction, which is jurisdiction over civil cases arising under the U.S. Constitution, an act of Congress, or a treaty, and diversity jurisdiction, which is jurisdiction over civil cases filed based on the "diversity of citizenship" of the litigants, such as between citizens of different states or between U.S. citizens and those of another country, in which the matter in controversy has a sum or value that exceeds $75,000. 28 U.S.C. §§ 1331, 1332.
[311]Pub. L. No. 380, § 2, 39 Stat. 1132 (1917).
[312] Carty v. Beech Aircraft Corp., 679 F.2d 1051, 1054 (3d Cir. 1982) (citing Ordinance enacted by Colonial Council for St. Thomas and St. John, Dec. 8, 1921 and Ordinance enacted by Colonial Council of St. Croix, Aug. 6, 1921).
[313]*Id.*
[314]*Id.*
[315]*Id.*
[316]Pub. L. No. 749, §§ 28, 29, 49 Stat. 1807, 1814 (1936).
[317]*Id.* § 28, 49 Stat. at 1814.
[318]*Id.* § 25, 49 Stat. at 1813.
[319]Pub. L. No. 517, § 22, 68 Stat. 497, 506 (1954).
[320]*Id.* §§ 22, 23, 68 Stat. at 506.
[321]*Id.* § 23, 68 Stat. at 506.
[322] 1976 V.I. Sess. Laws 188. The local court was reorganized and renamed several times. In 1957, the three police courts were combined into two municipal courts: the Municipal Court of Saint Croix and the Municipal Court of Saint Thomas. In 1965, the two municipal courts were combined into one municipal court: the Municipal Court of the Virgin Islands. In 1976, the name of the Municipal Court of the Virgin Islands was changed to the Territorial Court, and in 2004, the name was again changed to the Superior Court. V.I. CODE ANN. tit. 4, § 2 note; *see also* Government of the Virgin Islands v. Bryan, 738 F. Supp. 946 , 948 (D.V.I. 1990).
[323]*See* Government of the Virgin Islands v. Bryan, 738 F. Supp. at 948.
[324]1981 V.I. Sess. Laws 260.
[325] Diversity jurisdiction is described in 28 U.S.C. § 1332 and includes jurisdiction over civil actions in which the matter in controversy exceeds the sum or value of $75,000 and that are between citizens of different states, citizens of a state and citizens of a foreign state, citizens of different states and in which citizens of a foreign state are additional parties, or a foreign state as plaintiff and citizens of a state or different states. 28 U.S.C. § 1332.
[326] Pub. L. No. 98-454, § 703(a), 98 Stat. 1732, 1738 (1984). A previous law had conferred upon the district court the jurisdiction of a bankruptcy court. Pub. L. No. 95-598, § 336, 92 Stat. 2549, 2680 (1978).
[327]Pub. L. No. 98-454, § 703(a), 98 Stat. at 1738.
[328]*Id.* The law provides that the District Court of the Virgin Islands has concurrent jurisdiction with the local court over offenses against local law that are "of the same or similar character or part of, or based on, the same act or transaction or two or more acts or

Samoa Political Status Study Commission. Its primary recommendation mirrors the declarations of the previous political study commissions calling for the retention of the current relationship with the United States. The slight difference is the Commission's urging to continue the dialogue with the United States hoping to establish a permanent political relationship which affirms the protection of our land tenure system while eliminating jurisdictional impediments retarding our ability to become self reliant and self-sufficient. The Commission's report, which presents its findings and recommendations, is published and distributed to government leaders. The Governor is calling a Political Convention for November of this year to review, discuss, and issue recommendations of issues to be presented to the people of American Samoa for a decision in a referendum.

Before articulating the position of the Senate regarding the issue under consideration, allow me at this time to commend the recent report GAO-08-655 prepared and issued by the Congressional GAO Office on "Issues Associated with Potential Changes to the Current System for Adjudicating Matters of Federal Law". This document did an excellent job highlighting significant issues connected with each documented possible presence scenario for the Federal Court System in American Samoa. The report also acknowledged receipt and review of the content of the Public Hearing Report conducted on the subject. The overwhelming consensus of those present at the public hearing, organized by the Legislature of American Samoa, was to maintain the current status of our present Judiciary System. This same spirit is again expressed and echoed by the Senators and the Senate of American Samoa during recent deliberations attempting to determine the appropriate course of action regarding the matter under consideration.

The GAO Report laid out three principal scenarios for change, if a change to the current system were made: (1) establishing a district court in American Samoa pursuant to Article IV of the U.S. Constitution, (2) establishing a district court in American Samoa that would be a division of the District of Hawaii, or (3) expanding the federal jurisdiction of the High Court of American Samoa. The Senate concurs with some of the documented reasons which compelled the current assessment of the sufficiency of our present judiciary system regarding adjudication of matters of federal law. Despite this acknowledgement, the Senate is of the opinion that the problem is not systemic but more administrative in nature, thus the recommended solution involving federal court presence in American Samoa might be excessive given huge financial demands and other considerations. Similarly, the question of sufficiency of workload to warrant the fulltime presence of the federal court system, along with the annual financial demands to maintain the operation requires meticulous review. The GAO Report acknowledges substantial financial demands connected with the implementation of each of the three scenarios.

The Senate holds the view that that there are insufficient significant reasons why the establishment of a Federal Court presence in the Territory of American Samoa is merited. Nevertheless, the Senate is not opposed to the necessity to realistically assess whether our people have open and seamless access to justice on issues under federal jurisdiction. The Senate is also of the opinion that the majority of disconcerting legal issues are being adequately addressed by our existing judiciary system except for a few matters arising out of misappropriation of federal grants and human trafficking. It is unfortunate that the GAO Report did not prepare a fiscal comparison between the current costs connected with the present adjudication of matters of federal law and the cost of establishing a permanent federal presence in American Samoa. In the long run, it would be cheaper to maintain the current approach to adjudicating matters of federal law with minor modifications. This prognosis is predicated on our conviction that the number of violations of federal law will be reduced substantially. The painful lessons and our peoples' actual exposure to the workings of the Federal Bureau of Investigations supply sufficient deterrent precluding replication of such practices. We hold the belief that those who perpetrate violations against federal laws deserve the treatment they may received or encounter. The issue of human trafficking emerged more from our inexperienced to deal with such issues then deliberately attempting to perpetrate such gruesome acts.

We are not unmindful of the fact that the presence of the Federal Court System in the Territory will contribute positively to the Territory's economic attraction, as the perception for enhanced security of investment is raised. Moreover, the speed at which the adjudication of issues of federal law will be much faster. Nevertheless, the fear embedded in the loss of our lands eclipses the associate economic benefits inherent in the establishment of a Federal Court system in American Samoa. This fear might be baseless, but we have experienced painful consequences of foreign policy decisions. We understand fully the current realities especially when we weigh the interest of 67,000 inhabitants of American Samoa against the needs of approximately 284 million residents of the United States; obviously the interests of the majority will prevail. It is this reality which continues to fuel our fixation and obsession to do everything necessary to appeal for special consideration for the preservation of the indigenous elements of our culture and traditions that give credence and legitimacy to our ethnicity, identity, and way of life. Our land is the basic foundation of our cultural traditions.

We hold the firm belief that the current deliberations on the advisability, feasibility, and necessity for a federal court presence in American Samoa are premature. We noted earlier that the Territory of American Samoa has activated the process dedicated to assessing the sufficiency of its current political status relationship with the United States. The first phase of the process is completed culminating with the issuance and distribution of the 2006 American Samoa Political Status Study Commission Report. The Governor has invoked the execution of the second phase with the call to convene a political convention facilitating the review of the findings and recommendations of the Commission. The expected outcome of the political convention is the identification and approval of issues to be presented to the people of American Samoa for a decision. The expressed wishes and desires of the people reflected in the voting outcome will officially be presented to the Department of the Interior and the Congress of the United States. We deem the above described process to constitute the logical progression of events to get us to the point at which issues such as the federal court presence can be accommodated within the established framework similar to the Organic Acts of Guam and USVI, or the Covenant for CNMI. It is important to recognize that the Federal Court presence in Guam, CNMI, and USVI are clearly defined in formalized documents of political association or relationships such as an organic act or a covenant. This opportunity should be afforded to the Territory of American Samoa. The process is in motion to answer the question of political relationship sufficiency to accommodate modern day challenges while safeguarding national assets such as land and cultural traditions. This attempt aims to better define our formal relationship with the United States mirroring the contents of the formal political structures defined in an Organic Act or Covenant establishing parameters within which interfacing with the United States will be regulated. It does not appear prudent for American Samoa to piecemeal changes which might retard our future ability to fashion a political union with the United States that is reflective of our aspirations.

Our first plea for consideration by the Subcommittee, Honorable Chairperson Christensen, is to grant us the chance to complete our political status review process which is in motion; the results of which will accurately express our people's wishes and desires. The 2006 American Samoa Political Status Study Commission issued as its primary recommendation to maintain our status quo but then extended the proposal calling for continuing to explore and negotiate with the United States Congress a permanent political status. It is obvious and plainly transparent that the accepted wisdom behind this recommendation is to forge a relationship with the United States which will guarantee the perpetuation of our land tenure system and the latitude to ascertain direct financial and incentive commitments to bolster the expansion of our economic development capacity. We earnestly implore the Honorable Subcommittee to please let us canvass the will of our people particular to the type of political framework they deem beneficial to address issues affecting their quality of life. We envision the preparation of formalized documents similar to an organic act or covenant clearly articulating the political union with the United States representative of the wishes of our people.

In excess of 100 years, American Samoa's political status has been defined as "an unorganized and an unincorporated" territory of the United States. It is unorganized because American Samoa does not have an organic act or a covenant approved and ratified by the Congress of the United States defining parameters regulating internal and external interfacing with the federal government and foreign countries. It is unincorporated because not all federal laws are automatically enforceable in American Samoa. This political status relationship has served us well and continues to receive overwhelming support for its continuation. This sentiment is inscribed in the 2006 American Samoa Political Status Study Commission's primary recommendation. Since 1950, the Department of the Interior has maintained absolute power over the administration of American Samoa. Political changes experienced by American Samoa were orchestrated by the Department of the Interior. The agency has direct influence over American Samoa's judicial system, not only through its appointive powers for the High Court justices, but also serving as one of the integral stages of the appeal process. To address the noted concerns of the Department of Justice relative to aggressive prosecution of federal law violations, the Senate recommends that the Department of the Interior be compelled to place a federal prosecutor in American Samoa to immediately address the Department of Justice's concerns and expand the authority of the High Court to adjudicate matters of federal law. The High Court of American Samoa is already authorized to handle cases involving the violation of federal laws. This scenario will provide needed time for us to complete our political status review process. The Senate shares the belief that this recommendation is within the purview of the Department of Interior's overall mandate to improve the Territory of American Samoa's capacity for self-reliance and self-sufficiency. This change can easily be implemented without much doing, and it can be simply undone upon completion of the territory's search for a more perfect union with the United States.

In the event the Subcommittee deems the above two recommendations unfeasible, the Senate would endorse the third scenario involving the expansion of the federal jurisdiction of the High Court of American Samoa. This option eases to some degree our anxiety over the potential adverse impact of the federal court presence to our land tenure system. Additionally, we would like to include additional safeguards endorsed in the 1996 draft legislation to ensure clear understanding that matters pertaining to land and titles will never be addressed in the Federal Court System. Our preference is to incorporate these prohibitions in a revised constitution of American Samoa along with a lucid description of the preferred status of association and relationship with the United States of America. We would advocate for American Samoa to consider revising its constitution, after the political status review process is completed, incorporating the desired political affiliation with the United States, along with other issues, such as Federal Court presence, deemed necessary to clearly define said association and then have the Congress of the United States consider and ratify it as the official organizing document with the same force as an Organic Act or a Covenant.

The Congress of the United States has in retrospect made amends recognizing the rights of the American Indians and the sovereignty of the American Indian Nation. As such, ownership of their lands is secured and the utilization of said lands is theirs to do as they please. We are loyal Americans aspiring to obtain the same level of acknowledgment granted to the American Indians and the autonomy of its nation. Our loyalty to the United States of America is exemplified by holding the highest rate of voluntary enrollment per capita in the Armed Forces defending envied democratic values, and the unpleasant distinction of holding the highest per capita casualty and mortality rate.

Thank you very much again for this rare opportunity to offer testimony on legislation which extends Federal Court presence to American Samoa. While the question of the guaranteed perpetuation of our land tenure system is unresolved, the posture of caution will always be adopted when issues which potentially affect our lands and our inherent way of life are raised.

In: American Samoa: Federal Law and Court... ISBN: 978-1-61761-938-0
Editor: Lucas G. Ramos

Chapter 3

STATEMENT OF SAVALI TALAVOU ALE, SPEAKER OF THE HOUSE OF REPRESENTATIVES, BEFORE THE HOUSE SUBCOMMITTEE ON INSULAR AFFAIRS

Honorable Madame Chairperson Donna Christensen and illustrious members of the Subcommittee on Insular Affairs, I wish to convey to you greetings from the members of the House of Representatives. Opportunities of this nature are very rare indeed so I am certainly honored to have been extended the invitation to appear before this Subcommittee to present testimony on the issue of federal court presence in the Territory of American Samoa. The Federal Court System presence in American Samoa is an issue that is not new, as pointed out in the GAO Report and endemically acknowledged. Whatever the varying perspectives might be, the inherent intentions and expected outcomes are deemed merited, for the basic premise appears to be the comprehensive accommodation of our judiciary needs.We would be an ungrateful people if we fail to recognize and appreciate the attempt to mitigate issues of cultural sensitivities and ensuring that the justice system is adequately encompassing to guarantee full and impartial adjudication of matters of federal law. While our testimonies may seem hostile towards efforts aimed to establish a 'win win' scenario, between the federal government and the people of American Samoa, with regard to the principal focus on the difficulties of adjudicating matters of federal law arising in American Samoa, and due to American Samoa's remote location, along with the desire to provide American Samoans more direct access to justice, increased federal court presence is feared because of its possible adverse impact on our land tenure system and our way of life. However, be confident that we are appreciative of the efforts of the federal government, attempting to fine tune our justice system, giving surety to the protection of individual rights.

Notwithstanding our deepest gratitude over the advancement of the issue regarding federal court presence in American Samoa, the undercurrent obsession attached to the possible destruction of our land tenure system is so intense that logical and impassive exchange is difficult to attain. These are natural emotions because our lands and our culture are extensions of us, and any attempt at alteration means changing our people's DNA.This fanaticism provided impulsion and the catalyst compelling our forefathers to deed our sovereignties to the United States and expecting from the same the maintenance of the prevailing land tenure system, culture and traditions, indigenous to the inhabitants of Tutuila and Manu'a. These sentiments are being memorialized in the 1900 Treaty of Cession of Tutuila and Aunu'u and 1904 Treaty of Cession of Manu'a. Irrespective of the attitude of the United States, with respect to the inherent commitments expected to advance social, economic, and political welfare of our people, the leaders of the islands of Tutuila and Manu'a made and held these presentations sacred, anticipating that these similar sentiments are mutual. The relinquishment of sovereignties of Tutuila and Manu'aIslands were not byproducts of warring conquests or hostile occupation, but through peaceful acquiescence, with full expectation that the United States Government will honor the primary elements of the two Deeds of Cessions involving the preservation of the land tenure system and promoting social, economic, and political welfare of the inhabitants of the islands.

On April 17, 2008 Tutuila and Manu'a commemorated and celebrated 108 years of affiliation with the greatest country in the world. We take great pride in our association with the United States. This pride continues to flourish instead of dissipating. As a person privileged to be a member of the 2006 American Samoa Political Status Study Commission, I was exposed to the unanimity of expression of support for the continuation and perpetuation of our present relationship with the United States. As zealous as our pledge to the continuation of our connection to the United States is, so is our passionate support for the perpetuation of the current land tenure system and traditions. The most vociferous of response from the community on the question of political relationship with the United States is to maintain our present union, yet with the caution to hold on to our system of land ownership. We cannot discount or forget the goodness of the United States, because for 108 years, the basic elements of our two Deeds of Cessions have been honored and preserved. We can not skirt the issue inherent in our desire to continue to maintain this relational format. However, we would be delusional to think that the strength of the 108 years of harmonious co-existence will withstand the test when the fundamental democratic principles are applied to our land tenure system.

We are indeed indebted to the Congress of the United States for public recognition of the two Treaties of Cessions entered into with the inhabitants of Tutuila and Manu'a as memorialized in Title 48 of the United States Code, in which the endemic expression of desire for the preservation of our land tenure system is acknowledged. We share the thinking that this special provision is possible only because of our informal political relationship with the United States, being an "unorganized and unincorporated" territory. The experience of Guam and the Commonwealth of Northern Mariana Islands with respect to the alienation of their lands, perpetrated by the passage of the Organic Act and Covenant, is one we do not wish to replicate. The inhabitants of these insular areas are all U.S. Citizens, and it appears to us that the alienation of their lands is the sacrifice they were willing to make to acquire the privilege and inherent benefits of U.S. citizenship. It is clear from the testimonies received by the 2006 American Samoa Political Status Study Commission that the people of American Samoa are not willing to surrender their system of land ownership.

The 2006 American Samoa Political Status Study Commission made a point to physically visit some of the flagged territories of the United States with varying political statuses. Invariably, the residents of these islands lauded and expressed envy over American Samoa's current political relationship with the United States. This knowledge bolstered our confidence and affirmed our belief that opting to preserve our land tenure system and cultural traditions is the best possible option for American Samoa. We are also not oblivious to the disadvantages associated with this decision memorialized in the primary recommendation of the 2006 American Samoa Political Status Study Commission. In essence, the recommendation reaffirms the conclusions of the two previous political status commissions, calling for the adoption of the status quo posture. The additional stipulation to the recent Commission's recommendation is to continue the process for political status determination until the most perfect union is found. The perfect union envisioned by the 2006 American Samoa Political Status Study Commission is one which assures the perpetuation of our land tenure system and the elimination of economic development barriers precipitated by our present political status relationship with the United States. American Samoa is economically hamstrung because it lacks eligibility to access the financial services of the World Bank and the Asian Development Bank. American Samoa cannot participate in Pacific Organizations and forums comprised of independent countries of the Pacific as an equal partner, thus suffering exclusion from programs of regional flavor or fund leveraging activities with our Pacific Island neighbors because of our political designation. American Samoa's access to foreign aid is prohibited although our neighbors in the Pacific, like the Independent State of Samoa, Tonga, etc., are receiving developmental aid from other metropolitan countries of the World. These are but a few examples of economic impediments confronting American Samoa which the Commission has identified and used as the basis for the call to continue negotiations with the United States until the most practical and beneficial union is found and adopted.

The 2006 American Samoa Political Status Study Commission has exhaustively explored all the issues of significance upon which predicated its resulting recommendations. The Governor is presenting legislation for consideration by the Legislature calling for the convening of a political convention in November of this year, to afford the opportunity to the community to review the report and recommendations of the Commission. It is expected that this review will culminate with the identification, prioritization, and approval of issues and recommendations to be presented to the people of American Samoa for a decision in the form of a referendum. It makes logical sense to allow this process to run its course without externally induced complications to ensure that the outcome is truly reflective of our people's aspirations and desires. The plea is therefore made herein to suspend discussion on the federal court presence issue and allow us to complete the planned process for the consideration of the issues and recommendations presented by the 2006 American Samoa Political Status Study Commission.

The above plea also addresses the concern over the piecemeal changes applied to our judiciary system, caused by actions of U.S. Citizens demanding satisfaction of their constitutional rights. For example, the fear of not having sufficient population from which to draw an impartial jury because of close ties, has been rendered inconsequential and moot with the Circuit Court decision affirming Mr. Jake King's claim that his rights to trial by jury of his peers have been violated; hence the introduction of trials by jury. Moreover, there are already provisions of federal laws that are being adjudicated in the High Court of American Samoa. Throughout the 1960s and 1970s, and again in the early 2000s, federal law also provided that the High Court has jurisdiction over cases arising under certain other federal statutes. For example, the High Court has been granted jurisdiction over cases arising under certain federal statutes governing grain standards, pesticide control, animal welfare, animal and plant health, and poultry and meat inspection.These actions have the effect of shrinking potential political relationship options or force decisions that are not in the best interest of our people. The High Court of American Samoa has been given full litigation and adjudicative capacity to address any type or manner of white collar crime perpetrated against the American Samoa Government irrespective of the source of funding. We assert therefore that American Samoa's current judiciary system possesses the required legal scope to competently address matters pertaining to federal law and the need to change has not been clearly determined. The reasons given to change American Samoa's judiciary system, except for the associate cost, are not of sufficient merit to warrant and legitimize transformation.

The assessment conducted by the GAO Office documented in the GAO-08-655 American Samoa Report was thorough with lucid comparisons of judicial systems for Guam, CNMC, USVI, and American Samoa. The report also provided three possible format options for federal court presence in American Samoa. The report neglected to recommend one more option which calls for the maintenance of our present judicial system. Clearly, insufficient compelling reasons exist to warrant the adoption of one of the three options recommended in the GAO Report unless it is a foregone conclusion that judicial system change for American Samoa is inevitable. In any event, the GAO Office did an exceptional job bringing to light all necessary and relevant information upon which a prudent decision will hopefully evolve.

In the order of priority, preserving the current status of our judicial system is our preferred choice and should be our only choice. However, it is highly idealistic to think that passionate pleas alone are enough to sway Congress to heed these petitions deemed by the indigenous inhabitants to be reflective of their aspirations and desires. We have raised the issue relative to the significant issues compelling the movement to change the current judicial system in American Samoa. Except for complaints from the federal agencies connected with the judicial process, respecting the difficulty associated with the full discharge of their duties and the cost, we have not been privy to any grievance filed citing dissatisfaction questioning the integrity of the justice system and the quality of court decisions. We have also addressed our concern over the piecemeal manner with which federalism is being introduced into the territory without first settling the political relationship with the United States. The overall consequence of the current approach has the effect of truncating potential political status options which could be adopted by the territory to which best fit the aspirations and desires of the people of American Samoa. The recommendations of the 2006 American Samoa Political Status Study Commission are promulgated in its published report awaiting review and action by the community leaders of American Samoa; the decision from which derives possible political options to adopt will be placed before the people of American Samoa for a decision. This process is evolving with our Governor declaring the convening of the Political Status Convention for November of this year. Our hope and wish to complete this local process before any federal intervention is also placed before you for your consideration. For 108 years of association with the United States, our people have, in unison, opted for the continuation of our "unorganized and unincorporated" status. The compelling reason precipitating this unified declaration remains unchanged which is affirmed by the 2006 American Samoa Political Status Study Commission's primary recommendation to hang on to our present status. The addendum to the recommendation acknowledges the need to boldly address the issue of our land tenure system.

In the event our wishes are deemed insufficient to induce a favorable response, it is the general preference of the members of the House of Representatives to adopt Scenario III in which the High Court of American Samoa is empowered to hear matters of federal law. The implementation of this option should not pose a problem because the High Court of American Samoa is currently adjudicating certain matters of federal law. Trial by jury of ones peers is now a matter of law. This piecemeal change to our judicial system raised grave concerns and the implications of which were afforded attention in the earlier section of this statement. The additional uneasiness caused by this change is the process deployed from which this modification was derived. It took just one dissatisfied, and unhappy U.S. Citizen to forge the change, leaving us with no assurances that the same strategy will not be utilized to challenge the constitutionality of our land tenure system in the federal court system. Based on this experience, it is necessary to identify local issues which can not be adjudicated in the federal court system. While the adoption of Scenario III is the alternative choice, incorporation of language to allay our concerns over the vulnerability of land tenure system is requested and it should be made an integral part of the scenario.

Although cost associate with the three potential scenarios for federal court presence in American Samoa is an important factor, it should not be the principal determinant for the viability of each of the options. If cost is the controlling criteria, status quo would prove to be the most cost effective alternative. Our people have been consistent in expressing their desires and wishes to preserve their land tenure system and their cultural traditions.

We have also been unyielding and relentless in the contestation of proposals deemed to threaten the perpetuation of our way of life entrenched and embedded in our lands. We clearly understand the political pressures brought to bear on your shoulders to ensure that the rights of all U.S. Citizens are not compromised. Nevertheless, we are a small community far removed from the mainstream, struggling to maintain indigenous elements upon which it draws its identity as a people and a race distinct unto itself. This ideology does not diminish our patriotism nor lessen the pride we treasure as being Americans. Thank you for the opportunity to offer statement on the issue of federal court presence in American Samoa which has far reaching implications on our survival as a people.

In: American Samoa: Federal Law and Court… ISBN: 978-1-61761-938-0
Editor: Lucas G. Ramos

Chapter 4

STATEMENT OF STEPHEN SANDER, ACTING DIRECTOR, OFFICE OF INSULAR AFFAIRS, DEPARTMENT OF THE INTERIOR, BEFORE THE HOUSE SUBCOMMITTEE ON INSULAR AFFAIRS, HEARING ON "FEDERAL COURT OPTIONS FOR AMERICAN SAMOA"

Madam Chair and members of the Subcommittee on Insular Affairs, thank you for the opportunity to testify on Federal court options for American Samoa.

BACKGROUND

Fa'a Samoa

The people of American Samoa have always shown supreme concern for the preservation of *Fa'a Samoa*, the Samoan way of life.*Fa'a Samoa* is rooted in communal land ownership and the *matai* title system of American Samoa.It was the preservation of the communal land and *matai* systems that prompted the leaders of American Samoa in the 1950s to establish the foundations of their government under an order of the Secretary of the Interior.Included was a court of last resort, the High Court of American Samoa.A Federal District court was not established on American Samoa for fear that it may harm *Fa'a Samoa*.Issues relating to *Fa'a Samoa*, communal land ownership and *matai* titles, are as critical and relevant today for the residents of American Samoa as they were sixty years ago.

Federal Legal Issues and Structure

The issue of Federal court jurisdiction for American Samoa has arisen on numerous occasions.In the mid-1990s, after the publication of a report on white collar crime in American Samoa, there was a serious effort within the Department of Justice to develop legislation that would establish a Federal district court in the territory.However, no action was taken by the Congress.

Recently, at the request of Congressman Faleomavaega, the U.S. Government Accountability Office produced a report entitled, *AMERICAN SAMOA Issues Associated with Potential Changes to the Current System for Adjudicating Matters of Federal Law*.The report provides an excellent historical account and presents options for dealing with issues of Federal law.

The report includes a number of reasons for establishing Federal court jurisdiction in American Samoa:

(1) Increased prosecution of worthy criminal cases by eliminating current logistical obstacles (high travel costs between Hawaii and the territory, infrequent flights, and the inaccessibility of witnesses for testimony and trial preparation),
(2) Crime deterrence,
(3) Alleviation of embarrassment and costs associated with a defendant being removed to Hawaii for trial, and
(4) Collection of debts owed to the Federal government.

The report also outlines three possible scenarios for establishing a Federal judicial presence in American Samoa:

(1) Federal court in American Samoa similar to those in other U.S. territories,
(2) A Federal court in American Samoa that would be a division of the District of Hawaii, and
(3) Expanded Federal criminal and civil jurisdiction for the High Court of American Samoa.

FEDERAL JUDICIAL JURISDICTION

It appears that there are two questions:Whether or not Federal judicial jurisdiction should be established in American Samoa?And, if a Federal judicial presence is desirable, what form should it take?

The Department of the Interior has no objection to a system that more efficiently considers issues of Federal law relating to American Samoa.Such a system should be backed by the people of American Samoa through expressions of support from the leaders the American Samoa Government.In instituting any changes the Department of the Interior believes that it will be important for Federal judicial jurisdiction not to include authority over the American Samoan communal land tenure and *matai* systems.

With regard to the structuring of a Federal judicial presence in American Samoa, the Department suggests that the Subcommittee give full consideration to opinion from American Samoa concerning the structure that best would meet the needs of both the Federal government and the territory.

Chapter Sources

The following chapters have been previously published:

Chapter 1 – This is an edited reformatted and augmented version of a United States Government Accountability Office publication, report GAO-08-655.

Chapter 2 – These remarks were delievered as testimony. President Lolo M. Mogliga, before the House Subcommittee on Insular Affiars.

Chapter 3 – These remarks were delievered as testimony. Savali Talavou Ale, Speaker of the House of Representatives, before the United States House of Representative's Subcommittee on Insular Affairs.

Chapter 4 – These remarks were given as testimony on September 18, 2008. Stephen Sander, Acting Director, Office of Insular Affairs, Department of the Interior, before the Subcommittee on Insular Affairs, House Committee on Natural Resources, regarding Federal Court Options for American Samoa.

INDEX

U

V

W